M000158273

Prai...

"This book is a soft, sweet hand that will guide you to rest in the place where possibility is born."
— **Dawna Markova**, author of *Spot of Grace*

"An early writing prompt encapsulates the splendor, creativity, and power of Meredith Heller's new book: riffing on a Black spiritual, 'Dem Bones,' Meredith has us envision a 'sacred wound,' in which the heart bone is connected to the wound bone, the joy bone connected to the truth bone, the truth bone connected to the wisdom bone, etc. Through her masterful exercises and suggestions, Meredith guides us in making our wounds into sources of strength and connection, opportunities for peace, personal insight, and emotional growth. *Writing by Heart* expands our 'hearts,' as well as our 'writings,' through poetic mastery and a sense of belonging."
— **Stephen Rojcewicz, MD, PhD**, Distinguished Life Fellow of the American Psychiatric Association and past president of the National Association for Poetry Therapy

"Meredith Heller has written another exciting and inclusive soul-speak book. *Writing by Heart* provides a loving and passionate invitation to connect to our own life experience as if our stories, longings, dreams, and heartfelt, handwritten words matter not to just ourselves but to each other. Her generous sharing of everyday people's poetry allows us to feel connected and inspired to engage with our feeling self and write what we know from heart to hand to communal voice. As a spiritual psychotherapist and life coach, I bring Meredith's books into my practice as a tool to help us uncover our truth through the sacred act of writing."
— **Deborah Meints-Pierson, LMFT**, coauthor of *Love Tools for Everyday Heroes*, author of *Shelter in Place*, and cohost of the *Soul Path Sessions* podcast

"Meredith Heller invites us on a wild-hearted adventure to express our full-bodied truths. Weaving together powerful themes and playful practices, *Writing by Heart* catalyzes our creativity and calls us to befriend ourselves and share our treasures. This important and beautifully written book turns writing into a feast for the senses and the wild imagination."

— **Rebecca Wildbear**, author of *Wild Yoga: A Practice of Initiation, Veneration & Advocacy for the Earth*

"What a glowing gift! *Writing by Heart* is a luminous lamp lighting your writing way inward and forward. This is a captivating and wonder-filled book, overflowing with wild wisdom for your words to become known to you, and find holy homes in other eyes, ears, hearts, and souls."

— **SARK**, artist, author, inspirationalist, PlanetSARK.com

"Pick up your pen and lock your doors — you'll be excited to write! Meredith Heller gathers and provides vibrantly playful, innovative, effective tools for applied creativity as somatic healing agent. Drawing from her vast interdisciplinary training, experience, and courage, her accessible, fiercely nurturing guidance provides relentless dynamic support and hums through these pages — caressing, alchemizing, liberating our psyches."

— **April Heaslip, PhD**, mythologist, educator, and author of *Regenerating the Feminine* (forthcoming, 2024)

"The words *thank you* cannot capture the enormity of the gratitude I feel for this book. Meredith Heller's loving wisdom and encouragement leap from the page. Her students' poems call out like an incantation, a summoning of creative magic: *Join us with your voice, your words, your poems. You can do this!* When Meredith offers her prompts to 'Write Now!' my heart sings back, *Yes, yes, yes!*"

— **Heather Clague, MD**, coleader of the Feeling Great Book Club

Writing by Heart

Also by Meredith Heller

Songlines

River Spells

Yuba Witch

Write a Poem, Save Your Life

Writing by Heart

A POETRY PATH TO HEALING AND SELF-DISCOVERY

Meredith Heller

Foreword by John Fox

New World Library
Novato, California

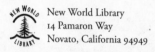

New World Library
14 Pamaron Way
Novato, California 94949

Copyright © 2024 by Meredith Heller

All rights reserved. This book may not be reproduced in whole or in part, stored in a retrieval system, or transmitted in any form or by any means — electronic, mechanical, or other — without written permission from the publisher, except by a reviewer, who may quote brief passages in a review.

The material in this book is intended for education. No expressed or implied guarantee of the effects of the use of the recommendations can be given or liability taken.

All student poetry used with permission.
Text design by Tona Pearce Myers

Library of Congress Cataloging-in-Publication Data

Names: Heller, Meredith, author. | Fox, John, author, writer of foreword.
Title: Writing by heart : a poetry path to healing and self-discovery / Meredith Heller ; foreword by John Fox.
Description: Novato, California : New World Library, 2024. | Includes index. | Summary: "Poet, writer, and educator Meredith Heller provides inspiration and invitations anyone can use to explore, express, heal, and find belonging through the power of their own words"-- Provided by publisher.
Identifiers: LCCN 2023049585 (print) | LCCN 2023049586 (ebook) | ISBN 9781608689101 (paperback) | ISBN 9781608689118 (ebook)
Subjects: LCSH: Poetry--Authorship. | Poetry--Therapeutic use. | Poetry--Psychological aspects. | Self-actualization (Psychology)
Classification: LCC PN1059.A9 H456 2024 (print) | LCC PN1059.A9 (ebook) | DDC 808.1--dc23/eng/20231023
LC record available at https://lccn.loc.gov/2023049585
LC ebook record available at https://lccn.loc.gov/2023049586

First printing, February 2024
ISBN 978-1-60868-910-1
Ebook ISBN 978-1-60868-911-8
Printed in Canada on 100% postconsumer-waste recycled paper

New World Library is proud to be a Gold Certified Environmentally Responsible Publisher. Publisher certification awarded by Green Press Initiative.

10   9   8   7   6   5   4   3   2   1

To you, brave heart

I write to discover. I write to uncover.
I write to meet my ghosts…
I write because it is dangerous, a bloody risk,
like love, to form the words.
— TERRY TEMPEST WILLIAMS,
Red: Passion and Patience in the Desert

I choose… to loosen my heart until it becomes
a wing, a torch, a promise.
— DAWNA MARKOVA,
from "I Will Not Die an Unlived Life"

Contents

Foreword

My heart wants roots, my mind wants wings.
— E. Y. HARBURG

Since 1982 I have dedicated my life to the healing power of poetry and poem making. I haven't cruised along. For each of those forty-three years I have paid attention to what is occurring in this remarkable, planet-wide, healing field.

I am committed to the growth and development of my work — growing organically the many ways poetry makes a healing change in people's lives. When I say it happens *organically* I mean that the success and the good happen because I make real connections and nurture relationships that are, that must be, more than me but are not separate from me.

My way is to continually realize I am part of something much more immense.

This is about being open to what and who is living in this expressive landscape. I am glad I am confident enough not only to allow for the success of others but also to be deeply open to and interested in the exciting work that others are doing.

Rilke wrote in his *Book of Hours: Love Poems to God* (as translated by Joanna Macy and Anita Barrows):

I know that nothing has ever been real
without my beholding it.
All becoming has needed me.
My looking ripens things
and they come toward me, to meet and be met.

Now I am going to share a profound meeting prophesized in these two lines:

My looking ripens things
and they come toward me, to meet and be met.

Who has come toward me to be met and to meet? That is why I am writing to you!

Two years ago an astonishing, amazing woman, Meredith Heller — teacher, poet, writer, healer, soul force, embodiment of life — appeared in my Facebook feed. That day I became aware of her book *Write a Poem, Save Your Life*. I bought her book, started to read it, and knew right away — *Meredith Heller had written a breakthrough book.*

I wrote to her immediately to offer praise and appreciation.

Soon she and I were in conversation about how the Institute for Poetic Medicine (the nonprofit I founded in 2005) could help fund the work that Meredith felt inspired to do. Our conversation, with the support of the IPM board, turned into actual funding for a range of programs to serve people at the margins — including women in a Minnesota prison.

Over the past two years, I've watched what she has done, and my admiration for Meredith — for her brilliant, profoundly creative ways — has grown and flourished. When she asked me to write a foreword to this new book, *Writing by Heart*, it was easy to say yes.

The introduction to *Writing by Heart* includes these words: "Each class is like a living organism." Reading this sentence, my instantaneous thought was that the book you are reading here and now is truly and wholly *a living organism.*

These are not merely words to get you to like this book. I mean them with all my heart. Meredith writes in this way — she mindfully, carefully, creatively, and wisely designed and structured this book so that each page is part of a living, breathing organism.

Writing by Heart is a body with bones, skin, musculature, blood lines, nervous and endocrine systems. A living organism that communicates health and is a catalyst for creativity.

This book is human. This book is spiritual. This book is community. *Writing by Heart* draws these dimensions together into a whole. This is what the world needs now, and Meredith hears and feels this great need. Reading the following words in her book helps me trust her: "Our culture is in a soul deficit. We have lost our circles, our communities, and with them, our sense of belonging." It is so true! *Writing by Heart* happily steps into that breach and delivers belonging to us.

This is key: the most important thing about this book is *you.* That is to say that while the human, spiritual, and community dimensions matter, the focus of this book, the welcome it expresses, the listening you can expect to find in it are for you and your actual life.

Meredith expresses this sense of personal welcome in sweet, comforting ways. In more than one place she says, "Get comfy," and "Close your beautiful eyes and settle in." We need more sweetness like this: I tear up to hear someone tell me I have beautiful eyes. I don't think anyone has ever written that in a book.

This book does not avoid hurt and suffering, which all living organisms experience. Yet because Meredith is a healer, you can trust that fertile ground can be found here, as well as a creative immune system; both will help you do what you are meant to do — lean into becoming whole.

One of the superb sample poems found in these pages includes these lines by Mary Pritchard:

> I plant my heart broken open
> freeing my pain and love and tears
> inviting others to join me in my truth.

I invite you to plant your "heart broken open" into this book, which was written to serve as a catalyst for your own poetic voice and creativity. This is not a book to read cover to cover. Instead, I recommend that you *use this book to help you slow down*. Take your time with a few pages; focus on a section at a time.

The true heart of this book are the questions Meredith steadily offers you to consider. This is another place of trust for me, trust in Meredith, trust in this book. Her questions are a plumb line helping me drop within myself. Her lean-into questions are humble and more creatively useful than those asked by someone who takes a stance of expertise. To use the ancient axiom about writing a poem: Don't tell, *show*. I could also say, Don't tell, *ask*.

This book overflows with show and ask. *Writing by Heart*, which is, by the way, a joy to read, is for you.

John Fox
Founder of the Institute for Poetic Medicine
Author of *Finding What You Didn't Lose:*
Expressing Your Truth and Creativity through Poem-Making

Introduction

A seed neither fears light nor darkness but uses both to grow.
— Matshona Dhliwayo

Welcome to *Writing by Heart*. We are about to embark on a journey into deep self, a wild and wonderful journey to help you discover your heart, your truth, your voice. And there's no wrong way. There is only you, discovering *your* way. Step by step, word by word. An adventure! Let's get started.

What does "writing by heart" mean? Well, I've always loved the concept of doing something by heart. When we do something by heart, we do it with an organic knowing in our bones and blood. Whether it's reciting a poem, singing a song, or walking a forest trail, knowing it by heart means we've made it our own. It has become part of us, like a friend. We can trust ourselves to know it, and we can trust that it will be there when we need it. My hope for you is that this poetry path becomes just that, a path of trust, in which you befriend yourself and your writing, and that it leads you home.

I had a yoga teacher who used to say, "This is not a yoga perfect, it's a yoga practice." So allow me to whisper in your ear as you write, "This is not a writing perfect, it's a writing practice." There's no goal to attain, no perfection to achieve, nowhere to get to, and no one to impress. Writing practice is about showing up and being present with yourself, however good or bad you feel. Noticing what arises for you, here and now, with curiosity and kindness. Your pen is the key and your paper is the door. Put your pen to paper and open the door. What's on the other side of the door? Your stories, poems, songs, ready to spill forth. Writing is a practice of trust. I like to say that the poem knows the poem. I promise that the more you write, the more fluent you'll become in writing by heart. You will learn to touch your truth, turn the past into compost, unearth juicy insights, and point the compass of your heart in any direction you choose. When you put your pen to paper, you will reap the harvest of your hardest lessons, tap the fountain of your wild wisdom, rebirth and reinvent yourself again and again as you weave your disconnected parts back into healing and wholeness. Because writing is magic. Writing is medicine.

As you journey with this book, you'll feel the companionship of the many women writers who attend my workshops. You'll read their poem-stories and become part of our circle. Circle and story are ancient, sacred containers for women's wisdom. Women have always gathered in circle around the fire, at the river, or at the kitchen table to share our experiences. We thrive on connection and cross-pollination. We learn and grow through osmosis and mirroring each other. We naturally entrain to each other. And we are emboldened in each other's presence. Yet our culture is in a soul deficit. We have lost our circles, our communities, and with them, our sense of belonging. This book is your invitation to come join us around the fire as we delve into the wild and beautiful mystery of ourselves. You are welcome just as you are, in all your hot mess and glorious brilliance. We are all in a state of transformation. Each of us is on a quest to discover and embody our passion and our purpose, to learn how to be true to ourselves, how to navigate love and loss, and how to share our unique genius with the world.

I know you've got a story to tell. I know there are words curled under your tongue, poems humming in your hands, incantations bubbling in your belly. I know there are manifestos in your laughter, love songs in your tears, rants and raves in the swing of your hips, song lyrics spilling out your back pocket — let them speak! Stories are alive. By writing our stories we bring out all our many separate threads, the frazzled and frayed ones, the sturdy faded ones, the luminous ones, the ones that throw sparks, and by warp and weft, we weave ourselves back into belonging. Grab your journal and pen, your curiosity and kindness, and meet me here in sacred circle to write and share your stories and to listen as others share theirs. Through writing we learn to trust that our experiences, no matter how challenging, are the soil from which we grow and bloom. Come dig in the garden with us, nourish your heart in the company of other writers, and allow the healing power of poetic writing to remember you back into wholeness.

I began writing in my teens. It was my lifeline. Writing was the way I lassoed the wild animals of my feelings, wrestled with my loves and losses, climbed through the bog of my depression. Writing was my refuge and my birthing ground. It's how I found my voice. You can read more of my journey in my first book, *Write a Poem, Save Your Life*. Indeed, writing saved my life, and I have witnessed it save many other people's lives over the past twenty-five-plus years of teaching poetic writing. I'm a firm believer in no mud, no lotus, but we can all use a helping hand. So here I am, mud-covered, scar-studded, wild-eyed, and singing at the top of my lungs — *grab your pen and paper and follow me!*

I've taught as a Poet in the Schools for more than twenty-five years, first in Boulder, Colorado, and then in Marin County,

California, using all the creative ways I know to help kids access and express their feelings, through writing, music making, and movement. Each class is like a living organism. What emerges is an organic flow and synergy in which universal themes emerge to be birthed, healed, shed, and shared, as we learn to navigate this human experience. What I've learned is that curiosity and love are the way through. I now teach workshops for adults: online and at women's prisons, creativity summits, and wellness retreats.

This book is the fruit of these workshops. The gardeners are the fiercely loving poet warriors who show up each week for workshop and write their hearts out. You will meet these warriors in the example poems in this book, and they will break your heart open. Workshops are multigenerational, populated by a range of people from their green twenties to their seasoned eighties. Some of them are new to writing, while others have been writing their whole lives. Our elders share from experience, while our youngers remind us how to see with new eyes. I have witnessed people show up for workshop imploded by the weight of the world and not knowing how to get in touch with their feelings and express their truth. What they find in workshop is an experience of being welcomed, accepted, and celebrated. They get inspired to dig in and discover their treasure. They learn that they are enough, that they are resourceful, and that their voice matters.

I invite you to join us, to practice writing about what's up and what's real for you. Write to digest your past, inhabit your present, and imagine your future. Write to tap the wisdom and metaphor that live and breathe beneath the surface. Write to compost what no longer serves you, and to bloom with renewed vitality as you embrace the inevitable ups and downs of your life. Come now, these pages are doors. Open any of them, and write yourself home.

CHAPTER I

Get Your Poetry Groove On

Gather the essentials for your poet's toolbox.

What *is* poetry? I use the term *poetry* to encompass all forms of expressive writing. As you use this book, feel free to write in any form you like: poetry, prose, essay, story, mind-spill, song lyrics — or make up your own form!

When I ask adults what poetry is, they say things like "words that follow a particular structure, rhythm, and perhaps rhyme," "a way of saying things slant," "using metaphor," and "writing in a descriptive and imaginative way." And these things are all true. But when I ask kids what poetry is, they nail it by saying, *feelings!* I would say all poetry, much like music, begins with a feeling, something that moves us deeply, fills and even consumes us to the point where we can no longer hold it and we spill open into expression. I like to use the analogy of a photograph. If I were a photographer, I would document my life by taking pictures of all the important moments that move me, capturing the full range of emotions, from devastation to joy. As a writer I do the same thing but with words. I want to remember and convey the feeling of a moment that touches me so deeply that if I'm lucky, it transforms me. Translating feelings into words: this is poetry.

Say Yes!

Say yes, and trust what arises as you write. You're building a relationship with your writing and your creativity. There is no wrong way to write and no wrong way to be creative. Creativity has a life of its own. And cycles. And tides. Invite it in. Say hello. Write down everything that comes to your mind, the ideas, images, feelings, sensations, memories. These are the gifts. Write them all down. You can get rid of what you don't want or need later. Give yourself permission to welcome whatever rises to the surface for your attention. It comes for a reason. It wants to be known. Be curious. The more you say yes, the more trust you build between yourself and your muse, or your creativity, or your intuition, or whatever that wild and beautiful thing is within us that feels called to express itself.

Write for yourself. Don't write for anyone else. Write to access your thoughts and feelings, to open a conduit to deep psyche. Write to learn something you didn't know you knew. Surprise yourself. Speak your truth, spill your secrets, clean out your wounds, touch what makes you sob and celebrate. Write yourself dark, light, sad, giddy, naughty, nasty, shy, miserable, yearning, elated, alive. Write yourself broken, open, whole, and holy. You are welcome here. *All* of you. This is your journey. Write from your experience. Write about what's really up for you right now. No sugarcoating, no tying it all up with a bow. Tell it real and raw. Be true to yourself.

Cultivate Your Writing Practice

Create a comfy, beautiful, private, inspiring writing space for yourself. Make a writing nook, a she shed, a witch wing, a bitch barn. Just do it! Bring pillows, candles, crystals, your journal and pen, a cup of tea, dark chocolate. Most important, bring *you*!

We have full lives. It can be challenging to make time to write, but what a gift to give ourselves. If you like routine, set up a schedule. Write in the morning when you wake up or at night before you go to sleep. Make time on the weekend. If you prefer to write by following your nose, create a more flexible approach by keeping an eye, ear, and heart tuned for what moves you. When something does, grab it by the tail and write it down before it gets away!

Tell your story. Say what's hard to say, what you've kept secret, what has lived in shame and shadow. Write about what hurts, and write about what you love. Write about what's scary, exciting, edgy, evocative, devastating, revealing. Write about what you feel, what you need, what you desire. Commit to not knowing ahead of time what you're going to write. Trust yourself. Trust the mysterious process of writing. The less you know, the better! This is how your writing becomes a living thing, a place of discovery.

Writing is about building a friendship with yourself. It is a way to access and integrate your life experiences. Writing is a mirror, a temple, a treasure box, a companion, a refuge, a place of alchemical transformation. Fulfillment comes from discovering something you didn't know you knew. It comes from developing your own voice and style. This takes practice, support, and experimentation. Be patient with yourself. We all have good and not-so-good writing days. Keep with it until it flows from your blood like a wellspring, until you'd rather write than not, because it feeds your soul, frees your feelings, expresses your longings, and helps grow you into the wildly beautiful and potent being you are. Just start. Write something crazy, messy, sad, shameful, dark, brilliant, bold, fierce, triumphant, sexy, irreverent, sassy, savage. Write to touch your core, bone-deep, where you sob and sing. Write to reach your own hallelujah!

Paper and Pen

An organic connection is made between body, brain, hand, and heart when we write with paper and pen. Give it a try. Writing with paper and pen is like dancing. It engages our whole being in a way that tapping away on the keys never can. Get a journal you like. It doesn't need to be fancy. I like a five-by-eight sketch pad with a spiral binding, so I can open it flat and fold it in half. I prefer unlined pages so I can doodle. I like a felt-tip pen that I don't have to push too hard to get the ink flowing. Experiment until you find what you like. Keep all your writing, and read back through it occasionally. I bet you blow your own mind. How did I ever come up with that?! Wow, I'm a good writer. Wow, I've been through hell and back. I'm a survivor. I'm resilient. Whoa, do I have some wild stories! Dig in and discover your treasure.

Writing Voice

Find your writing voice by tuning in to your unique way of saying things. It can be helpful to say things out loud and write them the way you say them. Read your writing aloud to yourself until you hear your own voice and cadence, the way you naturally express yourself, like when you're telling a good story to your bestie. Spark your own interest. Express your personality when you write. You don't want to sound like anyone else. You'll never be happy with your writing until you sound like you. Be true to your own voice. It's like your fingerprint.

Writer's Block

Ugh. Worst nightmare. Listen, it happens to all of us. My counsel is, don't fight it. Don't judge and annihilate yourself because of it. Simply acknowledge it. Yes, it sucks. It feels awful. You're afraid you'll never write again. You can't face yourself in the mirror. You feel hopeless. I know; I've been there. But pause, breathe, practice kindness with yourself. Think of it as a natural and necessary fallow time. Trust that whatever you need is composting and germinating underground, and that it will push up through the dark soil when it's ready. Change your environment. If you live in the country, spend a day in the city, or vice versa. Go outside. Move your body. Get your lungs and heart pumping. Walk, run, swim, bike. Put on some music and sing and dance. Take a nap, take a bath, embrace your downtime. Remember that everything is cyclical. Creativity happens in the in-between zone when we're not trying. Stories, poems, songs need time and space to birth and ripen. Trust me, the ideas will come when you immerse yourself in something else entirely. Let it go, don't think about what you're writing, allow your subconscious to work on it for you. Then, while you're having fun doing something else, have your phone or notebook handy, and get ready to catch the falling stars.

Metaphor and Simile

Metaphor and simile are poetic tools that connect two or more unrelated concepts and allow us to share a lot of information in just a few words, with an image to anchor it. For example, I can use a metaphor to connect my heart with a flower and tell you a lot about me with just a few words. If I tell you "my heart is a wildflower," that conveys different information than if I tell you "my heart is a rose." We draw on what we know about wildflowers and roses. When I use *wildflower* to describe my heart, you know my heart is resilient and hardy and grows wherever it's planted. When I say my heart is a rose, you know my heart requires special conditions to grow and thrive. Let's explore this more deeply.

Metaphor identifies; simile compares (using *like* or *as*; think *similar*).

For example:

Metaphor: My heart is a wildflower.
Simile: My heart is like a wildflower, or my heart is as resilient as a wildflower.

Metaphor: My heart is a volcano.
Simile: My heart is like a volcano, or my heart is as fiery as a volcano.

Metaphor: My heart is an ocean.
Simile: My heart is like an ocean, or my heart is as deep as an ocean.

Write a few of your own metaphors and similes describing your heartland.

Point of View: First, Second, Third Person

You'll want different points of view for different pieces, to express various perspectives. First person is the *I/we* perspective. It's close to home, personal, vulnerable. Second person is the *you* perspective. It's one degree of separation but also points to and includes others. Third person is the *he/she/it/they* perspective. It's like two degrees of separation, but it also allows us to see ourselves in others. Experimentation is key. Take a piece of your writing and try it in each point of view to see which one best conveys the feeling, ambiance, or message of the piece. Have fun with this.

Past and Present Tense

Try your piece in both past and present tense while you're writing or when you're editing. You never quite know which tense is going to bring your work to life. It's different with each piece. Play with it to find what works best. Read it aloud to yourself in past and present tense and see which one affects you more deeply.

Editing

There's a great line, "If I had more time, I would have written a shorter letter." (With a few variations, this line is attributed to Blaise Pascal, Mark Twain, and John Locke). Whoever came up with this quip, it speaks so aptly about editing. Editing takes time, focus, perseverance. You've got to sit with a piece of writing, chew on it, walk with it, breathe with it, sleep on it, puzzle it out twelve different ways until you find the melody and rhythm that ring. Is it ever done? No, not really. But there comes a point when you let go and accept that you've done your best with it for now.

My workshops and this book are geared toward generative writing rather than deep-dive editing, so you don't need to edit any of your writing as you work with this book or attend my workshops. However, if you want to try your hand at editing, two approaches I like are fleshing it out and boiling it down to the bones — or some dance of the two. Here's what I mean.

Fleshing It Out

Fleshing it out means using detail. Detail brings your piece to life. It makes it unique and memorable, personal and universal. For example, I can tell you I'm drinking a cup of tea.

Do you care? No, not really. It's OK, be truthful. But what if
I tell you:

> I'm drinking mint tea
> from plants I grew in my garden
> from a mug I made
> on a potter's wheel
> at my friend's studio.
> I glazed it with paint we made
> from crushed seashell
> and wood ash
> that we let dry in the sun
> before firing it
> in an earthen kiln.

Suddenly, this cup of tea got very interesting, yes? Detail, my
friend.

Boiling It Down to the Bones

Boiling it down to the bones means cutting away the extra,
the fat, the fleshy parts, the connective tissue. Getting rid of
everything you don't absolutely need until all that remains are
the bones, the essence. If I take my example of drinking a cup
of mint tea and boil it down to the bones, I might write:

> Mint tea
> garden grown
> hand-hewn mug
> wheel turned
> wood-ash glazed
> sun & sea
> earth baked.

What we're left with is just the essence, the bare bones, raw, potent, true.

Body/Mindfulness

I offer a Body/Mindfulness experience in each section of this book before we get ready to write. Think of it as a guided meditation, an invitation for you to sit back or lie down, get cozy, close your eyes, connect with your breath, and arrive in yourself here and now. You'll ride the waves of your breath into deeper presence as you soften and open to your inner world, deep psyche, and felt experience. Once there, you can source the feelings, sensations, images, ideas, and memories that will give rise to your writing.

Animal Guides

I began working with animal guides many years ago while studying shamanic journey work. It opened a world of inner resource that I turn to often for support and wisdom. I love sharing this journey work to meet our animal guides. All the experiences I've had with animal guides have empowered my life in a lasting way. Calling on the instinctual nature of animals leads us to transformative experience that helps us learn to source and trust our own wild wisdom. Throughout the book, I refer to these animal guides as allies, spirits, and totems. We'll commune with them to receive messages they may have for us. Often just being in the perceived presence of these animal allies brings us a deep sense of peace and companionship. By the time you work your way through this book, you will gather a whole council of animal allies you can go to for guidance. We all want to choose epic totems, like hawk and bear, lion and whale, but I suggest you allow your animal guides to choose you and trust who shows up. The smallest, most seemingly insignificant creatures can come to our aid with unimaginable resources. So if moth or honeybee, inchworm, ant, or mouse chooses you, welcome them and their wisdom with curiosity and gratitude.

Writing Can Stir Stuff Up

Because we often dig deep in our writing, it can stir stuff up: tough emotions, past trauma, loss, hurt, unresolved wounds. I believe our stuff surfaces to be healed. Hang in there. If you find you are overly stirred up from any of the writing you do, please seek professional therapeutic support to help you process and integrate. You are precious. Take good care of yourself.

How to Use This Book

Open to any chapter, read the theme, and do the Body/Mindfulness experience to deepen into presence, get in creative flow, and source deep psyche. Read the example poems; they will inspire you, I promise! Then follow the WRITE NOW! invitation. Not later, not at some other time when you're in the mood, but right now, whatever your mood. Jump in and write, now! Write for ten to twenty minutes, using paper and pen, if possible, and see where it takes you. If you love writing along with this book and want more support, contact me to attend an upcoming online workshop. Join a warm and growing community of writers, novice and seasoned. We have a blast. We laugh and cry. We get down and dirty, and we rise up, courageous and shining. You wouldn't imagine we could bond online, but we do. We inspire and support each other. We grow and find belonging together. I would love to have you join us: MeredithHeller.com.

CHAPTER 2

Elemental Wisdom

Harness the power of the elements to fuel your life.

The elements — earth, air, fire, and water — are living forces, potent with energy. Our ancient kin, they live in our bones and blood. If you doubt the power of the elements, go sit beside a river, hike a mountain trail, build a fire, feel the wind on your skin, breathe the air after a rainstorm, tune in to the rhythm of ocean waves. Earth, air, fire, and water each possess a unique power and wisdom, and we can call on their energy to help fuel our lives. Suppose we believe, as many aboriginal shamans do, that the four elements are alive and that the whole web of life is one interconnected organism. Then, like the shamans, we can ask for assistance with the cycles of life and death and harness these elemental powers to inspire and revitalize our lives. Let's open communication with the great organism of life and commune with our elemental allies as we draw on the different qualities each element offers.

Earth

Earth is associated with the body and the feminine. Mother Earth. Grounding. Fertility. Sensuality. Creativity. Cycles of growth and death. Let's begin by engaging with the earth element. Spend some time in nature. Walk barefoot. Work in the garden. Sit at the base of a tree. Lie down in the grass or the sand. Slow down and give yourself space and time to attune with earth's rhythm. Don't worry about what you're going to write; simply go outside (or look out a window) and be present with your experience of earth.

Body/Mindfulness: Find a quiet space to sit or lie down, close your eyes, and get comfy. Go outside if possible. Become aware of your breath, welcoming whatever rhythm or texture your breath shows up in right now, without needing to change it or fix it; just say hello to your breath. As you arrive more fully in your body and in this moment, feel into earth energy. What are you aware of? What do you notice and feel in relation to earth? What thoughts, feelings, sensations, and memories arise for you as you attune to the earth element? Call on earth and ask for its wisdom. What does earth know? What is earth's message for you? Give thanks to earth.

WRITE NOW!   *Write about your experience of the earth element. How do you feel when you connect with earth energy? What is earth's power or skill? What is earth's wisdom or message for you? What do you learn from the earth element that helps you at this moment?*

Examples

EARTH by Nicole Phillips

> When I stand in your
> fertile darkness

I feel deeply
nourished.

You draw me down
on reverent knees,
you tug my hands
into your gritty
moist crumbles.

You hold all of me —
the weight
the height
the chaos.

You accept me
you teach me
how to stay
how to pray.

Deep down
base layer
bass player
humming
me home.

EARTH by Lisa Eddy

Earth is strong and sexy
abundant and curvaceous
deep and dirty.

She is Mother
lover
friend.

She holds me
grounds me
feeds me.

She is rich
and wild
and free.

Earth
is
me.

Air

Air is associated with breath, spirit, inspiration, ideas, intellect. Air is the invisible net that connects us all. We all share air. Science says that all the air we breathe has been here since the beginning of life. That means we are breathing the same air that inspired the great mystics, musicians, warriors, artists, athletes, philosophers, writers, physicists, poets, storytellers, revolutionaries, environmentalists, lovers, and so many other luminaries who have walked this planet. We tend to take air for granted. Breathing too. Let's give thanks for the trees, the amazing beings who turn sunlight into sugar, carbon dioxide into oxygen. What is your relationship with air and with your breath? Breathe in and breathe out. Notice your breath as it fills and empties you. Breathing is always good medicine. Hold your breath for a moment and then let it go. Feel how your breath breathes you. Watch as your breathing mirrors your mood. Anxious, and it speeds up; calm, and it slows down. Do you tend to hold or release your breath when scared, angry, sad, excited? Just notice. Are you more comfortable inhaling or exhaling? Simply notice. Now let's engage with the air element. Go outside, if possible, and breathe and commune with the air. Don't worry about what you're going to write; simply be present with your experience of air.

Body/Mindfulness: Find a quiet space to sit or lie down, outside if possible, and close your eyes, get comfy. Find your breath and welcome whatever rhythm or texture your breath shows up in right now, without needing to change it or fix it; just say hello to your breath. Tune in to the air element. What do you notice? How does air make you feel? What is your relationship with air and with your breath? What thoughts, feelings, sensations, and memories arise for you when you commune with air? Call on air and ask for its wisdom. What does air know? What is air's message for you? Give thanks to air.

WRITE NOW! *Write about your experience of the air element. What power or skill does air contain? What is air's wisdom? What message or medicine does air have for you? What can you learn from the air element that helps you at this moment?*

Examples

THE AIR AT DUSK by Ani Meier

> You come winding through rock,
> through granite, silt & sand
> shaping arid valleys in my wake —

My mark, ahhh...
Dipping below into empty pools,
invisible river thrusting through matter,
the rigid, the "impenetrable" Arizona.

You seep in through dark & dank crevices
where you hide away from the sun's heat,
carrying the piercing eye of light.

I come to you now, ahhh...
I feel your urge to dance in colored skirts —
I swirl upward, spiral bidding you to dance
at the lavender edge of twilight
that traces my name in mountain Vs.

You are the wind thrusting forward on the freeway,
your guide, your launchpad & pedal.
Let me show you the world you're missing!

Ahhh... stop waiting...
You clear the sky of lizard clouds that disguise the stars,
the shooting star above Canis Major
that never fails to rain its praise on you
the moment you dare to stare.

Tonight you arrive in Sedona.
Greet me at 5 a.m. If you don't,
here I come breaking down the door.

THE UPDRAFT by Tiffany Fyans

Oxygen. Fire. Blood.
Mother's eyes, closed,
her children gather
gazing at the flame of her life.

Tank gauges, lines on screens
flicker behind
the rhapsody of her face
her everlasting beauty.

Circled around her
they feast on her pulses
her tongue at rest
stiff, white, still.

Mother's eyes flash open, clear
lock into each of ours in turn
speaking spirit to soul
imbuing her warmth
into our hearts.

Lighting us one by one
passing her fierce torch
melting all but love
in a final breath, shuddering
release.

The updraft of time
rushes through us
as her ember
flies into
eternity.

Fire

Fire is associated with life force, vitality, creativity, sexuality, and destruction. A person can be a firecracker, but they can also burn out or burn their bridges. Fire cooks our food and warms our homes, but wildfires, uncontained, are devastating. Every summer, here in Northern California, and around the world, including most recently in Lahaina, Hawaii, wildfires claim people's lives, homes, businesses, families, and pets. The loss is devastating. Of all the elements, fire is the one we have the least contact with, and perhaps it is the most mysterious. Let's engage with fire. Get ready to cook something on a gas stove, light the grill, make a fire in the fireplace or wood-burning stove, build a campfire, or burn a candle. Look at the flame, feel the heat, listen to the flame consuming what it needs to live. Tune in to the power of fire. Feel it? Don't worry about what you're going to write; simply be present with your experience of fire.

Body/Mindfulness: Find a quiet space to sit or lie down, close your eyes, and get comfy. Find your breath and welcome whatever rhythm or texture your breath shows up in right now, without needing to change it or fix it; just say hello to your breath. Feel into fire energy. What is your experience of the fire element? What thoughts, feelings, sensations, and memories arise for you when you commune with fire? Call on fire and ask for its power. What does fire know? What is fire's message for you at this moment? Give thanks to fire.

WRITE NOW! *Write about your experience with fire. What were you aware of while communing with fire? What power or skill does fire have? What wisdom can you gather from fire? What do you learn from the fire element that helps you at this moment?*

Examples

FLAMES by Lindsay Chinapen

> Orange sky rising
> ash falling from haze
> the remains of what could not escape
> the raging fire.
>
> Hot flames burn inside my chest
> filling me with anger
> trying to escape
> but with each heaving breath, it grows.
>
> I beg it to leave, but it won't.
> I want to control this fire
> I want to control the flames of my anger
> but she burns even hotter
> reminding me I have no control.
>
> My tears simmer the fire
> bringing her to a dancing flame
> breathe, I tell myself, breathe,
> and my breath dances with her fire.
>
> I ask her to burn away my anger and sorrow
> but she will not take it all
> for it is too entwined with my love.
>
> She says, "A flame must stay to remind you
> that you are alive with deep love.
> Your flame is love."

FIRE by Mary Pritchard

Flames of fire
igniting into existence
licking at my essence
searing my heart
scorching my reality
burning my life to ashes.

Fire, destroyer of life.
Fire, creator of life.

Rising gracefully
you reach out your arms to me
offering me warmth,
love,
healing,
hope.

Water

Water is associated with emotion, intuition, creativity, adaptability, pleasure, cleansing, and flow. We are watery by nature. Humans are about 80 percent water, as is the earth. Our fluids are pushed and pulled by the moon's gravity, just like ocean tides. Water is a shapeshifter. Flowing rivers, crashing waves, glaciers, steam. Water is said to be the strongest of all the elements, the way it wears a path for itself, drop by drop, slowly and patiently over time. Let's engage with water. Wash, splash, bathe, drink, water your garden, water your houseplants, wash your dishes, wash your car, go for a swim. Go and play with some form of water. Don't worry about what you're going to write; simply be present with your experience of water.

Body/Mindfulness: Find a quiet space to sit or lie down, close your eyes, and get comfy. Find your breath and welcome whatever rhythm or texture your breath shows up in right now, without needing to change it or fix it; just say hello to your breath. Feel into water. What is your experience with water? What thoughts, feelings, sensations, and memories arise for you when you commune with the water element? Call on water and ask for its wisdom. What does water know? What is water's message for you? Give thanks to water.

WRITE NOW! *Write about your experience of water. What is the power of water? What is water's wisdom and skill? What message does water have for you? What can you learn from the water element that helps you at this moment?*

Examples

WONDROUS WATER by Jeannie McKenzie

> Oh, incubator of life!
> Tides of dreams!
> You manifest in wondrous waves.
>
> Crashing and swirling
> parting and plunking
> following flows only the moon knows.
>
> My body, my blood
> pulse and flow
> rhythms of circulating currents.
>
> Tumbling down waterfalls
> twisting into hurricanes
> dripping in drizzles.

Holding still,
an iceberg frozen
through millennia.

Oh, wizard of changes
teach me the lessons
of adaptation.

School me
in shapeshifting
dip me to my depths.

So I too may flow
effortlessly
free from form.

WATER I AM by Nicole Phillips

Thank you, water
you allow me
to float disarmed,
you offer me
a holistic embrace,
you trace
my blood ways
with miraculous touch,
you hold me
neutral and uncomplicated,
you return me
to the womb.

Thank you, water
you remind me
of the dynamic

body of water
I am.

BECOMING ELEMENTAL

You've made friends with the elements and harnessed their power to fuel your life. Now allow me to guide you through an inner journey to merge with each element's energy until one of them chooses you and you become that element, embodied in its power, wisdom, skill, and beauty.

Body/Mindfulness: Cozy in and close your eyes. Allow your breath to breathe you in and out in tides. Feel yourself deepen and arrive inside as your body softens and opens. Place a hand on your belly and a hand on your heart to ground and support you as we journey to become each of the elements. Take as much time as you like with each element. You will know which one chooses you because you will feel it. Trust yourself. Here we go.

Earth: Imagine earth in your bones. Breathe with earth. Breathe with your bones. Allow yourself to become earth all the way down into your marrow. Welcome the feelings and sensations that arise for you. As earth, what is your mission? What is your power and wisdom? Who are you? How does it feel to be earth?

Air: Feel air in your lungs as you breathe in and out. Feel how the air fills and empties you effortlessly. Allow yourself to become air. Welcome what arises. As air, what is your skill? What is your power and wisdom? Who are you? How does it feel to be air?

Fire: Imagine fire in your heart. Let your heartbeat fan the fire. Feel the heat of the fire radiate through your whole body. Allow yourself to become fire. Welcome what arises for you. As fire, what is your mission? What is your power and skill? Who are you? How does it feel to be fire?

Water: Imagine water in your blood. Feel the fluidity of water as it moves through your whole body. Allow yourself to become water. Welcome the feelings and sensations that arise for you. As water, what is your power and wisdom? Who are you? How does it feel to be water?

Take a moment now and allow one of the elements to choose you. Notice which element feels most resonant for you, which one feels most alive, inspiring, nourishing, comforting. When one chooses you, give yourself completely to that element until you become it. Feel yourself as this element, solid as earth, light as air, hot as fire, fluid as water. As this element, who are you, and what do you know? What skills, power, and wisdom do you bring?

WRITE NOW!   *Write about your experience of becoming this element. How did you know this was your element? Why and how did this element choose you? What does it feel like to be this element? How do you move and express yourself? What do you need to thrive? What do you have to offer? How does being this element inform your life?*

Examples

I AM EARTH by Kelli Mulligan

> I arrived with a bang —
> I thump and clunk as I coalesce.

Burning hotter than fire, I rage,
release from my dark depths
as the weight of the sea fills my lungs
and drowns my fears.

I am caught in a gravitational tug-of-war
with my sun and moon.

They belong to me, and I belong to them.
We dance for all the beautiful souls.

I lean toward the light,
soaking up its electromagnetic rays
and it fills me with energy and loyalty.

I lean away from the light,
allowing my children to rest
and begin anew each year.

I AM AIR by Laurie McMillan

I am air because I am dancing into the open even when
the doors close. With my wind sister who always stirs
me from my home and asks, "Where is your home?"
Could it be with the wind and the way I am breathed
by the world and breathe out what I don't need? In that
exchange is essence, those ions that mingle in magic
dimension. They are my chalkboard upon which all is
written, all will be written. That's why I am packing
to go because I do not understand retiring into the
emptiness of a nest. Feathers need to spread. I draw from
wind sister knowing, intuition, and empathy because she
has seen what is not easily seen: suffering, joy, all that

hides in closure. The way I surround everything, fill the room, invisible strength, full of pressure, steady pressure is what I do. I smell of the unique scents from the field, mountain, and hot breath of desire that fills imagination with wonder. Wonder, the wings know wonder. Can you ride on wonder? Be wonder? Breathe wonder and grow purple wings. Yes. Yes. Flying in dreams, landing somewhere where I can speak to the dead who are living on, again the exchange is where I can grow, not in isolation. Air knows separation is an illusion. So many illusions. But that's OK. Picture riding on the magic carpet into a castle without doors or windows because the air is all in and out at the same time. All one. Imagine how light you can be through imagination, like breathing the air at a waterfall, this soul place of yours where the wings are made. Imagine yourself wearing a new set of wings. They are made of lace and memories, and a sky-blue shelter in the air. There's no place you cannot go. Go with me.

I AM FIRE by Natalie Keshlear

I am the crackle, and I am the pop
that lulls you to sleep
the warmth that cuddles up against your cheeks.

Red and pink, bringing flame to the surface of your skin,
I am blood, watering the ground beneath red-soiled feet
constellations between steps and among trees.

Dancing wildly in the middle of the forest
scar maps and bands of heat
energy and messiness.

Creating directions to the home place,
I am candlelight, incandescence, and restlessness
and staying up until dawn.

I am embodied and sweating and shaking wildly,
yawning, stretching, howling at the moon,
I am wolf. I am bear.

I am all teeth and fangs
and sleeping close in the den,
I am woman running wild. Run.

I am fox medicine. Intuition.
Stepping lightly
dancing on tippy-toes.

Seeing the details under the words,
between sighs, looking you straight in the eye,
I am ember and blaze.

Nourished from small to mighty
full of whooshes,
the power of believing.

I Am Fire.

I AM WATER by Verana Bailowitz

Clear. Fresh. Salty.
I move always, down & back
toward the lowest place
and here I rest
in this deep well

this dark cave.
Trickle. Droplet. Source.

Transparency. Incandescence. Reflection.
I am the wetness in my grandfather's eyes,
pooled there now in these last days of his life
I see myself reflected, coming & going,
youthful & aging, here & forever gone,
holding on while letting go
flowing always into the next tide.

Welling. Overflow. Downpour.
I am rush and wild torrent
the forever flow of waterfall,
white and blue and oh! The noise!
I scream into my own center.
Heard only by God, crash, and calm.
Bellowing. Liberating. Purifying.

I need only lean back
into the gentle current of my being
resting in & down
moving always toward the lowest
darkest place.

CHAPTER 3

Body Language

Let your body speak!

Write your way around the body, starting with your hands and moving on to your belly, hips, an area of injury, illness, or neglect, and then, yes, to your vagina, eeek! Listen deeply as your body opens to teach you its secret language, sharing its war stories and love songs. Sing the sagas of your feet, breasts, womb, a sacred wound, and finally end with a humorous or endearing ode to your tush! Let's do this!

Our bodies! Did you get the manual when you were born? No? Me neither. But I sure wish I had, don't you? All it would really need to say is: Welcome, I am your home while you're here. Take care of me, listen to me, trust and respect me, be grateful for me, and most important, love me! Bodies. These miraculous self-healing bio-homes through which we experience life and love. Our loyal life companions from birth to death. Most of the time we take them for granted. We push them, bruise them, break them, ignore them. We starve them and we stuff them. We judge and criticize them, relentlessly: too much of this, not enough of that. Most of us don't stop until they're wounded or broken, sick or exhausted. Then we berate our bodies for hurting and not doing what we need.

Our bodies are instruments with which we play the songs

of our pleasure and joy, strength and skill. But they are also reservoirs of pain and wounding, hiding and shame, unconscionable trespasses, and violation. Bodies are both battlegrounds and holy ground. Our bodies are the smartest, wisest, most self-healing organisms we will ever know. Let's take a moment to give thanks. Wrap your arms around yourself, give yourself a hug, and say thank you to your beautiful, resilient body.

It isn't always so easy to love our bodies, is it? I grew up at war with my body. Never good enough, strong enough, thin enough, athletic enough, beautiful enough, perfect enough. Sound familiar? Loving our bodies doesn't come naturally for most of us. The media portray women in ways we can rarely measure up to, making us focus on what we look like rather than on how we feel. Feeling good, feeling at home in our bodies is an inside job. It takes most of us a lifetime to come to peace with our bodies, to love our bodies. This journey of body love is essential and hard-earned. It is a path home. The body is instinctual. It doesn't lie. So when you need to make an important choice, ask your body. Belly knows. She will either relax and flutter open with a delicious yes or constrict into a fist with a definitive no. Let's open communication with our wise and wonderful bodies. Let's practice listening, trusting, and loving our bodies. Let's hold them with kindness when they hurt, gratitude when they heal, and celebration when they experience joy and pleasure. Welcome to your body.

Hands

We'll begin with our hands, a humble, essential, complex, and not overly vulnerable part of our bodies. What articulate and skilled creatures our hands! Each finger a sensitive tool in the clan. Our opposable thumbs an evolutionary miracle. With our hands we bring the world to us and shape it. Take a moment and look at your hands. Really look. Wiggle your fingers as you notice and name all the different parts of your hand: fingers, thumb, joints, knuckles, nails, palm, fingerprints. Think of all the things you do with your hands! Make a list. Surprise yourself. Even our language is full of colloquial hand-me-downs: you can lend a hand, try your hand, on the other hand, you sure are handy, this is a hands-on experience, my hands are tied, I don't need any handouts, I gotta hand it to you, you're a handful!

Body/Mindfulness: Sit or lie down and get comfy. Settle in and take a few breaths in your own rhythm. Allow whatever you're sitting or lying on to support you as your body softens and melts open. Now become aware of your hands. Squeeze them into fists, and then stretch them wide. Move your fingers. Say hello to these magnificent creatures. Now bring your hands together in any way that feels natural to you. You may hold your hands in prayer, or interlace your fingers, or clasp or cup one hand in the other. Allow your hands to sense each other and say hello, so that each hand feels held and experiences holding.

WRITE NOW! *Write an ode to your hands. The word* ode *is Greek for a poem or song that honors and celebrates something or someone. Acknowledge and sing the praises of your hands. Tell a story about your hands. The way you talk with your hands like your grandmother did. The way they knit or draw or play the piano or build things as if they have a mind of their own. How you caught fireflies or lizards in your hands when you were a child. Holding hands with someone you like. The time you broke one hand and had to learn to rely on the other. What stories are humming in your hands?*

Examples

MY HANDS by Heather Irene Bush

> My fingers touch the keys
> musical braille on my harmonium
> notes I could never read as script on a staff
> but could recognize by feel.
>
> When I was a kid, my left hand found it difficult
> to play something different from my right.
> Mr. Y, my piano teacher, gave me classical pieces to play,
> but it should've been the blues.
>
> I am deep emotion and evolving structure
> I cannot find myself in the acronym Every Good Boy
>   Does Fine
> I am intuitive and spontaneous, not neatly composed or
>   refined
> I am ragged, and I am raw.
>
> My hands too are raw
> my thumbs throb and bleed .
> my cuticles sacrificed to anxiety.
>
> My fingers hold regrettable cigarettes
> make copious cups of coffee in the morning
> before facing another day of pandemic.
> I grip my phone and wait for the dopamine to hit.
>
> Fortunately, there are no bass notes for my left hand on
>   harmonium.
> Instead, it pumps prana into the cardiovascular system of
>   the bellows
> controlling the volume and dynamics of sound.

My hands carry my heavy instrument to California,
 Mexico,
and up and down the filthy New Yok City subway stairs.

I miss Lily, my Chinese nail lady in Chelsea,
she used to massage my weary hands
with cheap cucumber lotion
before painting my bitten-down nails.
She knew my hands better than anyone in that lonely
 city
I wonder where Lily is now.

When I was a kid
I wrote messages to myself on my hands
sometimes I still do.

THE HAND I WAS DEALT by Heleen Ellmore-Walzer

At fifteen, dazzled by the long, lacquered fingernails
on the soft, sweet hands of my best friend
I slipped into the age-old practice of comparison
and landed on the cruel conclusion
that I hated my frail
not-good-enough
hands.

My nail beds
too short
robbed me of glamor.
Bitten, bloody,
ragged nails
evidence of my fear
the grip of my shame
distress at my fingertips.

Holding the forbidden black-and-white
snapshot of my dead mother
I study it
searching for clues
a discovery of who she was
aching for a truth I can live from.

I notice her petite hands
her short nail beds
clutching roses.

Belly

Belly up! Our bellies, the sensitive, intimate, soft or muscled area in the center of our bodies. The place of our belly button, where we were attached to our birth mothers by umbilical cord for nourishment, like a piece of fruit ripening on the mother tree. Now we tend to our own feeding by the feel of hunger or fullness in our belly. The gut is considered the second brain. Scientists have found that there are as many neurons in the belly as there are in the brain. We say, I've got butterflies in my stomach, a knot in my belly, quit your bellyaching. Belly is a place of truth and wisdom. Notice how your belly responds to what you're experiencing. Can you feel it tighten when things are a no-go and relax when it's clear yes? Do you trust your gut?

Body/Mindfulness: Sit or lie down, settle in, and get cozy. Place your hands on your belly. Breathe into your hands. Feel your belly fill and empty in and out of your hands. Say hello to your belly. What feelings arise as you give your attention to your belly? What's bubbling up when you tune in with your belly: anger, sorrow, fear, excitement, anxiety, hunger, shame, joy, longing, grieving, desire? What wants to be acknowledged in your belly? Without judgment, simply say hello, I'm here with you, I feel you, belly.

WRITE NOW! *Ask your belly some of the questions below, giving yourself permission to answer in any way that feels true to you. Yell, shout, vomit, spit, whisper, weep, sing.*

Belly Questions

- What are you angry about?
- What sadness are you holding?
- What feels exciting?
- What haven't you digested?
- What are you *really* hungry for?

Examples

BUDDHA BELLY by Indigo Donaldson

> My Buddha Belly
> is swollen with ideas
> and creative works
> yet to be shared.
>
> Some days it's full
> of undigested thoughts, feelings, and events
> I wonder if I can turn even the difficult ones
> into songs, poems, and stories
> give them my presence
> let that have precedence
> over hurt, fear, frustration.

I use my intention
to love my Buddha Belly
so full of goodness
and abundance
like a garden
overflowing with a ripe harvest
of nourishment so vast
it could feed the world.

PURGING FALSEHOODS by Heleen Ellmore-Walzer

I stuff my fingers
down my throat
forcing out a toxic
violent spew of
self-ridicule,
retching on shame,
undigested chunks
of self-disgust.

The hollow of my throat
is sour and sore
I plummet into a spell
of dry heaves
pressing and hurling
my way to the edge
of releasing what poisons me.

Longing for the eviction
I'm met with dizzying
refusal. My grip
on this venom runs deep,

generations deep
centuries deep
this poison is not all my own.

Sweet body,
I beg you to release
what doesn't serve you
I invite you to learn a new
language of love.

To transform self-shame
into self-pride
self-ridicule into self-respect
self-diminishment
into self-development.

Come, feast
on a banquet
of compassion.

Hips

Hips are the gateway to the wild. They move and respond with a life of their own — to music, lovemaking, physical work, carrying a child. Whether our hips move freely or are restrained in protection can tell us a lot about ourselves. If we've been violated, we tend to rein the hips in, like soldiers guarding the homeland. As we come to trust ourselves and life, we're able to let loose with our hips, moving easily, swinging down the street in graceful or even sassy figure eights. Most hips I've met harbor a rant or rave, usually a bit of both. Hips have a lot to say. Give them a chance, and they will rant against their mistreatment and rave about the glory of movement. What say your hips? Do they rant? Rave? A bit of both?

Body/Mindfulness: You can do this sitting or standing, or you can try it both ways. Put your hands on your hips and feel your hip bones. Then move your hips around, noticing how and where they move or don't. Do they swing easily from side to side, front to back? Can you draw figure eights with your hips? Is one direction more fluid than the other? Just notice. Do any places feel tight or get stuck? As you bring movement into your hips, notice what feelings, images, sensations, or memories arise. No judgment. Hips are potent terrain. Just say hello to your hips.

WRITE NOW! *Write about what you noticed while moving your hips. Are they a place of power and expression for you or a place of holding and protection? A bit of both? Is there a rant or rave your hips want to express? Tell the story your hips know. What happened that made them tight or free? How do they feel when they rock to the rhythm of music or lovemaking? Use any of the questions below to get started. Give it a swing!*

Hip Questions

- How do your hips feel when they move naturally to walk, dance, make love?
- Have your hips been shut down? How and why?
- What frees the movement of your hips?
- If you could name the attitude you carry in your hips, what would it be?

Examples

WHAT'S BETWEEN US by Natalie Keshlear

These hips
sometimes a separation
touching these hips
judgment, shame, competition
squeezing these hips
dark, dangerous, unknown,
alien hips.

Look at these hips.
Did you look?
See these hips and listen
a reawakening between these hips
wisdom in these curves
softness, strength
speaking in slow waves
up and down,
caressing these hips.

With an inhale and exhale
unraveling and blossoming
a becoming between these hips
a coming between these hips
an opening up
connection to creation
possibility, expansion,
between these hips.

These hips we share
beauty, power, scars,

stretch marks
sprouting up like roots
from me to you,
you to me.

Between these hips we move mountains.
Between these hips we speak truth to power.
Between these hips we are sisters.
Between these hips we collide.

BLOOMING HIPS by Lindsay Chinapen

Broad, bony, bruised
bumping into corners
attempting to figure out how to swing forty inches of leg
unknowingly converted into a dangerous weapon
leaving opponents bruised instead.

Hips rather ignored until high school,
the day you were out on display in spandex on the court,
for all to see, no charge for admission.
Face flushed, heat spreading in my body
swinging my legs quickly in my baggy basketball shorts.

My hips confused me
they were used only to propel me
in various directions on courts and fields
viewed as a structure until college.

And then: Wow! These hips can move!
Rolling, swinging, swaying to the beat of the music
sweat dripping down my body
my hips on display and it's OK, I like it.
Inviting his hands to join in their rolling circles.

Oh, these hips!
All that rolling, swinging, and swaying
led to carrying and growing two beautiful girls
widening more, making room for new life
protecting them, I get it now.

I finally understand you, but not until recently.
It's been a journey,
lessons of power, sexuality,
strength, and softness.

Hips, you are my feminine divine
where hot-pink azaleas bloom.

Injury, Illness, Neglect

If you have ever suffered with injury, illness, or chronic pain, you know how draining it is, how it dictates and diminishes your life. With injury we tend to block off from the injured area emotionally and physically. We withhold our breath and blood flow to these spots. We tighten, protect, and abandon ourselves at the point of injury so we don't have to feel the pain and loss. What if we could open communication with the parts of our bodies that are ill, injured, or neglected? For example, my left shoulder has always been tight, protectively pulled in toward my heart, and when I tune in and listen to my shoulder, just as it is without trying to change it, I feel its sorrow. What if I entered into dialogue with this sorrow? "Hello, sorrow. Hello, shoulder that holds sorrow. What has made you so? Would you be willing to tell me your story?" And then I offer my attention with curiosity and compassion. Have you neglected a part of your body because of pain, illness, or injury? Can you commune with this area now, inviting it to open and talk with you, as it learns to feel safe in your care and companionship?

Body/Mindfulness: Sit or lie down and close your eyes. Settle in and get comfy. Allow your body to feel supported by what's underneath and behind you. Invite your body to soften and melt open. Allow your breath to breathe you in whatever rhythm and texture it shows up in right now, without needing to change or fix it. Scan your body with your awareness and notice if there's an area that calls out for your attention because it hurts, it's injured, or it's an outcast. Perhaps it's been broken, overworked, overused, underappreciated, shamed; perhaps it's weak, had surgery, in pain, had limitation. Bring your love to this area and say hello. Invite it to share its story, its pain, loss, fear, sadness, anger, shame, grief. Listen to its story with great care. Tell it you accept it, you love it. Ask what it needs from you to heal, to be included.

WRITE NOW! *Write about the body part that has called for your attention and care. Tell the story of this body area. What happened there? What does this part of your body want you to know? What does it want to say? Is there something it needs from you? What does it feel like when you offer kindness, acceptance, inclusion? Can you talk to this body part as if it's your child or friend whom you love dearly? Write the story of this part of your body.*

Examples

DRAGON SPINE by Jeannie McKenzie

> The wedge in my heart
> worked its way

through my spine
with years of bulimia
pushing up
what wouldn't
go down.

Eating myself
eating to fill the emptiness
eating to fill the crack in my heart
the left side and the right side
taking sides
masculine versus feminine
active versus receptive.

Early media messages taught me
this body I was born with is not enough
not thin enough
not blonde enough
not straight enough
not masculine enough
not feminine enough.

So I tried to fit
twisted to fit in
twisted my guts
twisted my spine
swallowed and choked
by my own judgment
when more than anything
this spine wanted to ripple and sing.

Somewhere in this curvy spine
this beleaguered belly

lay a dragon birthing itself into being.
A dragon who could swim and swirl and fly
whose compassionate heart could hold space.
A dragon who could breathe its fiery breath
of acceptance, tenderness, compassion.

Breath by fiery breath
masculine and feminine
integrating
into my curvy
dragon spine.

THANK YOU, BODY by Hala Emad

Thank you, body, for being here
even though I was in another place.
You suffered a lot of pain
waiting for me.

Sorry, I am a bad person
who treats you like a neglected bag,
a bag for a busy mum,
full of things that she may need in the future.

You always deal with all my faults
with acceptance and mercy,
you speak to me even when I close my ears,
you whisper with love, scream with love!

Scanning you days ago,
I found a lot of weeping there,
a lot of unfinished work,
hungry emotions, and longing.

Yes, I miss me too.
I miss being with you, in harmony,
talking to you with compassion
listening to music and dancing with passion.

Sorry for all the days, months, years,
I was wearing another body in my dreams,
refusing to accept you as you are.
Sorry for all the great expectations
I made you deal with and pass their test.

Thank you for not leaving me
even when I wanted to leave you,
pushing you off a high mountain.

Thank you for respecting me,
for helping me to look strong,
even though we were so weak.
You swallow my tears and swell with them.

Thank you for being my friend,
my companion and lover
even when I hate myself.
Thank you for this long illness,
to rest my thoughts,
and bring me back to·pray.

Vagina Time! (Eeeek)

You didn't think we would do a women's body-language workshop without writing about our vaginas, did you? Because
if we didn't, I'd be fired from the vagina squad. So today is

vagina day, or as I used to say to an old lover of mine, "Guess what time it is?" And he'd say, "What time is it, babe?" And I'd say, "It's vagina time!" So it is. We are entering tender territory. Take your time. Approach with kindness and curiosity. Some of you may never have written about your vaginas, while others of you may have entire collections of ballads and love songs to and from your vagina. As with Eve Ensler's book and play, *The Vagina Monologues*, hearing and sharing our vagina sagas can be a liberating and bonding experience for women to give voice to all the stories, unconscionable and glorious, that we carry in our most precious place.

Body/Mindfulness: Sit or lie down now. Close your eyes. Cozy in and allow your breath to breathe you. If comfortable for you, place a hand on your heart and a hand on your vagina, and simply be present and breathe. Notice what arises for you when you connect with your vagina. Most of us have a strong mix of feelings, images, sensations, and memories, good and not so good. Is there anything your vagina wants you to know? A repressed memory? A desire never voiced? A story or secret ready to be told? Listen now. No judgment, just curiosity and kindness. Hello, my vagina.

WRITE NOW! *Read through the questions, storylines, and fun explorations below. See which one feels juiciest to you, which one wakes a story in you, or feel free to weave a few together. Make it your own.*

Questions

• What's it like having a vagina? (If you have a penis, what's that like?)

- How has yours been wounded? How has yours been loved?
- How did yours lose its power? How did yours claim its power?
- How or when did yours learn to say no? How or when did yours learn to say yes?
- What does yours like? How does yours choose to express or share itself?
- What names have you heard, used, or made up for your vagina? Here are a few examples to get you started: *pussy, cunt, coochie, precious, twat, snatch, fanny, yoni, vulva.*

Storylines

- My best or worst sexual experience was...
- My sexual desire is...
- What flames my erotic passion is...
- My secret fantasy is...
- The time my vagina experienced pain, wounding, rape, violation, or neglect...
- My vagina's favorite lover...
- My kink is...

Fun Explorations

If my vagina were a/an _____, it would be... (describe):

- Environment: desert, jungle, forest, estuary, ocean, etc.
- Animal
- Weather system
- Type of music or a particular song
- Food
- Flower
- Instrument

- Vehicle
- Foreign accent

Musings

- If my vagina dressed up, it would wear ...
- What famous artist would I choose to draw, paint, photograph, or sculpt my vagina?

Examples

V by Dawn Li

> V, you and I share many secrets
> sweet, bitter, juicy secrets
> midnight escapes
> swimming pool's glistening corners
> holding a foreign object
> that melted in my mouth.
>
> Then I vomited, no period for months
> I was afraid and blamed you
> I took you to a clinic
> the doctor opened you up
> and snapped at you
> as if for punishment.
>
> V, you gave me my first depression
> hallucinations of jungles and thunderbolts
> fighting bloodthirsty battles
> while your own volcano
> was kept asleep for years.
>
> Until one day, V became the *v* in *velvet*
> you were dressed in a silk gown

kissed, licked, and massaged
released to a wild beauty,
a phoenix.

Shivering a crescendo of pleasure
feminine force
from an ancient cave
rolls in with laughter
cracks open my bones
like an overflowing river.

V now becomes the *v* in *love*.

LADY LABIA by Heleen Ellmore-Walzer

I wear my vagina on my sleeve
she is my heart of hearts

Diamond light
soft center strength

Pulsating red with life
she leads the way

Sweet, sticky
honeypot of pleasure

Exquisite vulva
home of my explorations

Quivering mysteries
unfold among the folds

Clitoris, my queen
I bow to you

Again
and again

Sacred treasure
between my thighs
My beloved
My grace

Slow down
you whisper

With your tantric
yellow moonlight breath

Slowly. Gently.
What's your rush?

Savor this new rhythm
of presence

Move with tenderness
into the silver shadows.

Feet

Stand your ground. Find your footing. Tiptoe. Footloose. Live with a gentle footprint. Earthing. If the shoe fits. To truly understand someone, you must first walk a mile in her moccasins. Tell me about your feet. Where have they been? What's their secret? Do they like to be cozy in socks and shoes or bare and free? Tickled with a feather, massaged with strong thumbs? Do you squeeze them into strappy sandals, doll them up in heels, march them up and down mountains in leather hiking boots? Do you paint your toenails passion-red or mermaid-blue? Do you enjoy squishing them through mud or sand or garden soil? Do you take them out to dance? Do they ache? Do you have a high arch or flat feet? Do you feel the beat in your feet? Do you wiggle your toes in time to the music? Feet in or out of the blankets when you sleep? Favorite pair of shoes? Ever broken one of the twenty-six bones of your foot? Ever walked on someone's back barefoot? Ever walked across hot coals? Tell me about your feet. Step by step, word by word.

Body/Mindfulness: Sit rather than lie down for this one, please. Place your feet firmly on the floor, barefoot if possible. Close your eyes. Allow your breath to find you, without needing to change or fix it; simply surf the waves of your breath, in and out, as you come into deeper presence with yourself. Place your feet flat on the floor, feeling how and where they meet the ground. Which parts make contact, which parts are raised? Check in with your arches, your toes, your heels, and the outer edges of your feet. Without changing anything, just notice. Wiggle and separate your toes. Then take a foot in your hand and give it a squeeze. Hello, foot! Oooh, that feels good. Now open your eyes and look at your feet. Without judgment, simply see your feet. Take in all the details of these amazing creatures. If possible, get up and walk around the room, slowly, feeling how all the bones and tendons work synergically to press, push, lift, and carry you. What a symphony of cooperation, the human foot! Feel into the rhythm of this foot team, one foot and then the other, taking turns, balancing, as they move you around the room. Thank you, feet!

WRITE NOW! *Write about your feet. Describe them, their shape, texture, strength, skill, flexibility, pain, wounds, scars, anything that wants to be voiced. Tell the story of your feet, where they've been, what they've done, what they like or don't like, step by step.*

Examples

SOLE OF MY SOUL by Shea Morris

> I watched my mother walk miles to serve
> those who did not serve her.
> Her toes began to snarl and growl
> her tenacious tendons snapping like turtles
> rabid dogs howling under New Mexico moonlight.
> I followed in her footsteps
> shoving my feet
> toe by tender toe into bear traps
> heels so high, the altitude changed my breathing
> it's sexy they said, to walk like a newborn calf.
> I too walked paths of servitude on my stilts of insecurity
> my own stumps barking and tearing
> at the very sole of my soul.
> They did not deserve to be imprisoned for crimes they
>   did not commit.
> They deserved to be the pedestal at the base of my trunk.
> I learned how to bathe them in bubbles
> adorn them with rings and lavishly painted scarlet hues,
> ten twinkle-toed ticklish piggies,
> all headed home.

LITTLE ANCHORS by Sarah Barber

> so flat. which is one of the contradictions of this magical
>   bio-machine

because if there's one thing to be said about my body,
it's ... curvy.

how something so little can hold up something so fierce
is a mystery to me, so i don't ask too many questions.

so cold. how are my little anchors always. so. cold.
how my face will flush with lust or rage
my whole body burning except the little icicles that make
    the foundation
is a mystery to me, so i don't ask too many questions.

i'm a little person on little legs and little feet
walking in stride with people much taller than me
these flat little friends of mine have taken me to the tops
    of mountains,
the bottoms of rivers, through cobblestone streets, and
    onto my grandparent's lush carpet.

overworked and underpaid
with the thankless job of holding me up
taking me through
letting me be
walking me home.

Breasts

Breasts — soft feminine territory, a place of pleasure, pride, shame. Nurturing. Nourishing. Breastfeeding babes. Sensuous creatures that live on top of our chests, right here on top of our hearts, an extension of heart, perhaps? Our breasts are the first thing we meet the world with. The word *mammary* comes from the universal *mama* in all languages, *mama, mother,* the *mmmmm* sound most likely one of the first sounds uttered from sucking, *ma ma ma.* There are so many terms for breasts: *tits, boobs, boobies, points, knockers, bosom, bust, jugs, rack, squeeze box, bazongas, bazookas, balloons, bazooms. The girls, the twins, the assets.* The sad thing is, so many of us judge and compare them. Too small, too big. Too much. Not enough. Cleavage, no cleavage. Reveal, hide. Sagging. One's bigger, one's smaller. Breast(s) lost to cancer. Mammogram nightmares. And then there are nipples. Ah, nipples. We could do an entire workshop on nipples. And of course, bras: lace, underwire, push-up, camisole, no bra! Have you swum topless? Tell a story about your breasts, sad, sensual, celebratory. Budding to blooming. Pleasure or pain. How do they like to be touched or suckled? What word do you use to describe your breasts? If you could make up a new word or phrase, what would you call your orbs of delight? By the way, that's mine, *orbs of delight.*

Body/Mindfulness: Sit or lie down. Get comfy. Close your eyes and go inside. If you're comfortable, place one or both hands on your breasts. Breathe with your breasts as they rise and fall. Give a little squeeze to say hello. How do you feel about your breasts? Are they just right for you? Do you wish them to be different? Are they sensitive and erotic? How do they like to be touched? Did you nurse your babes? Have you altered your breasts in any way? Have you had breast reduction, implants, piercing? What's your relationship with your breasts?

WRITE NOW!   *Write about your breasts. Are they a place of pleasure, pride, joy, shame, hiding? Tell the breast story that wants to be told.*

THE ALTAR by Elizabeth E. Winheld

Many have bowed
at the altar
of my chest
but I will never forget
the sweet sounds
of my children nursing —
what a gift, to know that
my body could satiate like that,
bringing delirious pleasure.

And in those moments,
I finally understood
why children and lovers
bury their heads
in our chests and
why some men obsess
over bigger and bigger
breasts.

We are all trying to get home,
to find our way back
to that cradle of light,
that golden river
where our only job is
to receive love.

MY BREASTS by Sarah Barber

i have my grandmother's breasts and i'm grateful for that,
because it also means i have her heart. and her spirit.
i believe her whole upper torso was passed on to me
so i always get to keep her close.

a woman born before her time, fighting her way to
    college
even when that meant having to use the back doors of
    buildings
and stomach the backhanded compliments and front-
    handed insults
that she didn't belong —
ha. good luck.

i wear my breasts on my chest like a badge of honor.
a "don't fuck with me; do you know who my grandma is?"
kind of attitude that leads me into every room with
    undeniable power.
never have i seen mediocre white men more easily
    disarmed
than when i catch them stealing a glance.
such a direct transfer of power as their cheeks flush and
    words mumble.
shame. how does it feel?

in reality, i can't blame them.
i stare at this soft squishy army of two any chance i get.
i revel in the comfort i feel when i touch them.
the way my hand is drawn to them when i am
    overwhelmed
with love or gratitude, or grief.
i clutch them when feeling anxious or overwhelmed,
calling on the wisdom and beauty of the woman
before me who gave them their shape and weight
and whisper, "we're here. you're okay."

i'm grateful for this soft and comforting waterbed
that lies over my heart and keeps all its secrets safe.

i'm grateful for these two gorgeous layers,
given to me by my perfect grandma,
that protect my delicate heart
where i keep her.

Womb

Our wombs. Our dark gardens. The fertile space within us from which life arises. Generative and creative. We are connected by our wombs to the great mystery that brings forth life. Womb. Motherland. Great-grandmother country. We are tethered to the long bloodlines of our grandmothers by the eggs we are born with. We are all living matryoshka dolls. Life within life. Ovum within ovum. Woman within woman. The fact that women can produce new life is miraculous. We are special! Some of us have had children, one or many, some of us have lost children, and some have not birthed children, but perhaps like me you've birthed poems, songs, books, homes, gardens, relationships, work, and a life you love.

Say the word *womb* to yourself a few times, and listen to its ancient chant calling us home. Like an exhale, the *w* sound is a whoosh from the great spirit; the middle of the word contains the *om*, the sound of creation; the *o* is the egg, it is the fertile space of nothingness and all possibility; the *m* is *mama* and *yum*, and it ends with the soft but solid drumbeat of the consonant *b* that holds it all in place so it can root and gestate.

Our womb is a place that fruits our love and passion. But our wombs can also be places of loss, miscarriage, abortion, hysterectomy, wounding, scars, surgery, painful menses, menopause, and dreams that did not ripen. These stories are welcome here too. Your story. Herstory. Your womb is sacred space. It is the place where the great mystery creates through you. It is the soul soil from which we birth life, art, and all labors of love.

Body/Mindfulness: Sit or lie down. Close your eyes and climb inside. Allow your breath to breathe you in tides. Feel the support of what's underneath and behind you, so your body can soften and melt open. Place your hands on your womb area and say hello. Breathe into your womb and sense the energy that resides there. Connect with the mystery and power of your womb. Perhaps you feel heat, movement, swirling, bubbling, safety, stillness, silence. Commune with whatever is there. Try sounding into your womb area, like a low hum or moan, and notice what you feel. Say the word *womb* to yourself and feel into the primal sound of this word. Let it vibrate through you. What sensations, images, feelings, or memories arise for you as you attune with your womb?

WRITE NOW! *Write about your experience communing with your womb. What did you feel when tuning in? What energy lives and breathes in your womb? Did anything bubble up from your womb that wants your attention? Any desires or wounds that would benefit from your listening? What have you birthed, what are you birthing now, or what do you want to birth from the garden of your womb?*

Examples

MY WOMB by Sierra Tanner

> My womb.
> My womanhood.
> My home.

I should know you deeply,
but I don't.
Do you remember me?
Do I remember me?
Tell me your name,
sing to me while I sleep,
when the terror of your mystery doesn't grip my throat.
Sing to me in moments of pause,
when the pain of your blood stills me,
holds me close
and maybe then
your voice will guide me back to you.
Your voice,
both hymn and horror,
lures me in like a siren of the subtle.
One day,
when your song serenades me into surrender,
I will kneel willingly
at the altar of my destruction.
Go ahead,
devour me,
scour me until my soul shines
with the light that's been hiding,
waiting
for the reminder
that all of me is holy.

MIDWIFED BY SARASWATI by Jac-Lynn Stark

My womb no longer bleeds
but is not a desert or a dust bowl
pear-shaped space within my lower belly

no babies ever nestled there
curled in on themselves
instead, it nourishes different versions of myself
always wanting to be born
rebirthed and evolving
with fewer antilife messages
absorbed within my mother's body
from her fear-based life.

It is a waiting room
where what needs to be born
has time to ripen
and then come forth
sometimes in scraps of lines
scribbled on envelopes, shopping lists, receipts
then misplaced or thrown away by mistake.
Sometimes in dreams that fade quickly
leaving faint images on my internal retina
that I try to decipher
or barely discernible feelings
that haunt my waking hours
sometimes in tentative trial and error
incomplete beings that don't live long
but still have something to give me.
Sometimes in completed poems that start out messy —
lines, arrows, crossed-out words, marginal scrawlings
embryos of what they will become
with my own hard labor
over words, rhythm, meaning.

Some pour out like a fountain, an easy birth,
while some are slower to emerge
need to be induced

go through long painful labor
messy sweaty exhausting
before finally emerging
midwifed by Saraswati
goddess of creativity and wisdom.

Sacred Wound

Let's start by singing all the wounded parts home. Do you know the melody of the old song "Dem Bones"? Feel free to make up the words the way we do in my workshop: the heart bone connected to the wound bone, and the wound bone connected to the courage bone, and the courage bone connected to the hope bone, and the hope bone connected to the joy bone, and the joy bone connected to the truth bone, and the truth bone connected to the wisdom bone, and the wisdom bone connected to the moon bone, and the moon bone connected to the song bone, and the song bone connected to the poem bone, oh yeah!

We all have cracks in our bodies, places of wounding. The late great poet and songwriter Leonard Cohen said in his song "Anthem": "There is a crack, a crack in everything / That's how the light gets in." He echoed Rumi: "The wound is the place where the light enters you." We'll work with this concept as we enter a wound or crack in our bodies, bringing our warmth and love there, welcoming it back to the hearth of our bodies, and discovering how this crack helps us open so the light can get in. Some of us have many wounds, many cracks, so much light! Let's explore the power and medicine that hide in these wounded places and discover how we can make peace with them, bringing our loving-kindness there, so we can open and live more fully.

Body/Mindfulness: I invite you to light a candle to bring warmth and light to this wound, to offer it to the fire of transmutation, and to free up any stuck energy so you can open more fully to life. Look at the candle flame and breathe a few cycles of in and out while communing with the flame. When you're ready, close your eyes and breathe yourself into deeper presence with your body. Place a hand on your heart and ask your body which of your physical wounds could benefit from the warmth of your loving attention right now; then place your other hand there if possible. Say hello to this area. Breathe with this area. Let this wound know you are with it to offer kindness and support. Wait until you sense that it feels safe. Then invite it to express its pain and loss. Simply listen. No judgment, no blame. Let the wound receive your attention. If this is enough for today, then open your eyes slowly and begin to write about your experience. If you feel you are ready to dig deeper, then ask to understand how this wound presents an opportunity to soften and open, to let the light in. Does this wound help you grow compassion for yourself and others, point you in the direction of what matters to you, what you value, the gifts you came here to share?

WRITE NOW! *Write to honor the pain and loss of this wounded part. Allow the wounded part to speak if it wants. Then if you like, find the doorway in this wound that helps you open and take heart with yourself and others.*

Examples

SNAKE SCAR by Teya Valentina Chavez

> Hello, you,
> you were born when I was sixteen years old
> you are always with me.

You are like a strong mangled old tree trunk
that got cut into
the core of you
the core of me.

Three and a half inches of bone marrow
taken out of my left leg
and discarded,
where are you now?

After the surgery
I tried bringing you home
but they wouldn't let me.
This scar runs deep
deep into my core
smack in the middle
of my left femur.

They just
sawed
    me
down
    jagged
sad
    fault
line.

The car
hit me
flying through the air
nine-year-old leg,
broken
growth plate
shattered.

You, sweet snake-scar of mine
left hip serpent that sheds her skin
you bring me into presence with myself
with your shiny sparkling snake spirals
winding around the back of my leg
where my butt cheek and hamstring meet
at my inner thigh
down to the edges
of my left ankle.
And with each step
I am present
like a strong mangled old tree trunk.

EMPTY GAP by Lauren Montgomery

There was an empty gap,
where some Thing should be.
The sound of a single drip, drop
within a hollow cave.
I lit a fire there,
because I wanted to see
in the cold dark.
And it grew, my little fire,
setting off the alarms
of chaos.
The Out
of Control.

In my panic, I ran,
but my speed only fed the fire.
The fear was thick, and I choked,
my weighted conscience
a crown of thorns

the fetters of feminism
wrapped around my waist.

There was another thing there with me
in the dark,
a hungry animal,
also a very much afraid
starving, tired creature,
and I had only more
cold heavy fears
to feed her.

She wanted to be
full.
She appeared so ferocious
in this simple carnal need.
But I didn't remember how
or where, to find a little
nourishment.
Thick shame
that drove her
when she remembered how to eat.
Breaking free,
to gorge her hungry bones
on anything around.

My heart broke for her today
and in my hollow place
she had left
liquid light
spilling in
through the opening
she had torn in me.

Ode to the Tush

We have arrived at the tail end of the body language section. I say *tail* intentionally, because today we will write an ode to our tush! Yup, our tush! *Tush, booty, buns, butt, bottom, bum. Derriere, rump, rear, tuchus, fanny, ass,* just to drop a few names. We all have one, or is it two halves of one?! The gluteus maximus is one of the largest and strongest muscles in the body, yet like so many other body parts, we women measure them as too much or not enough. Ancient goddess art depicts woman as voluptuous, curvaceous, bountiful. Yet many of us drive ourselves crazy with diets and exercise to reduce or increase the roundness, dimples, or curves of our butts. Whether your rump is plump, your cheeks pretty as a peach, your booty bountiful, or your silhouette slim and svelte, be kind to your behind. Give your bottom a pat and a squeeze, be grateful for its power, purposeful and sensual. Take it out of hiding, and shake that thang. LMAO.

Body/Mindfulness: Sit or lie down, and get comfy. Close your eyes and allow your breath to breathe you into deeper presence. Give a wiggle to your behind as you cozy in. How do you feel about your buns? Are they an area of pride or shame for you? Do you try to diminish or accentuate your curves? Have you received praise or bullying for the size or shape of your bottom? Can you bring your loving-kindness and humor to this area of your beautiful body?

WRITE NOW! *Tell the story of your relationship with your bum. Have you always been on good terms, or has the journey toward embracing your derriere been edgy? Do you hide or take pride in your ass? Do you celebrate your curves? Admire your silhouette? Take your muscled moons out for a gallop? Do you shake* *it on the dance floor? Do you swang your thang while strolling through town? Tell it, girl!*

Examples

BUNDA by Aychele Hill

> Bunda, you are abundant
> *Abundância*
> There is a movement in your curves,
> a wave of pleasure.
>
> My grandmother pointed to my fleshy parts and said —
> You are a woman
> because your hips are large
> and you are made for carrying babies!
>
> I have always heard that large hips attract men
> because we are wired to make life, to make love.
>
> But media has a way of telling women
> that we need to change what we've got —
> this not-enoughness, this too-muchness.
>
> As a teenager, I heard the perfect ratio
> for a woman's body was 33-23-33.
> I have always exceeded that
> because of my abundance.
>
> My bunda is too big for this world!
>
> In my teen years, I tried to hide it
> under blouses wrapped around my waist
> while the boys at school would call me

Potranca, "Filly."
Potranca has *anca* in it,
which is also a word for hips.

I have always felt that my ass
is the most animal part of my body —
like a horse
or a zebra
or a gazelle.

This round, moonlike shape,
furry and bouncy.

Some lovers admire my stretch marks
calling them my tiger stripes
and as a tigress, I rejoice
in the little bites received in ecstasy.

My bunda,
you are a force to be reckoned with.

MY TUSH & I by Verana Bailowitz

I'm rather fond of my tush.
I take her everywhere.

Last week
I took her to a meditation retreat
and I sat with her
for eight long days.

My tush and I —
and my thoughts.

For eight long days.
We sat. We stayed.
All day long.
Perched upon my derriere
I sat. We sat.
My tush and I.

Thoughts arose.
What will I wear tomorrow?
I want to get a bite to eat.
I'm sad. I'm angry. I'm tired.
I want to stand and hike,
dance and sway.
I feel connected. Now I don't.
We watched my thoughts,
My tush and I
as they rolled in
and floated away.

My tush gripped when I attached.
My tush softened when I released.

I sat on my tush
and thought about life.
I sat on my tush
and thought about death.

Who am I?
What am I becoming?
How do I want to live?
How do I want to die?

My tush and I listened to dharma talks
about the four noble truths,
about dukkha, inevitable suffering,
the five hindrances to awakening,
about loving-kindness, compassion, and equanimity.

At times my tush went numb,
but still we sat, my tush and I.
Dissolving separation, layer after layer
letting go of things needing to be different,
my tush and I became one.

The more we sat,
the more I gathered myself in.
Here. I am here.
Me and my tush.
My tush and I.

CHAPTER 4

Sensorium

Awaken your senses!

In every moment we take in thousands of units of information through our sensory apertures: smell, touch, sight, hearing, and taste. We navigate the world through the synergy of our senses, guiding us toward survival and away from harm. To understand how crucial our senses are, try removing one. Go blindfolded or wear earplugs for an afternoon, and notice how this affects your capacity to perceive and interpret the world. We take our senses for granted, but they are our allies and informants. Let's dive into the world of our senses and discover how these essential instruments orient us with a sensual feast of information that directs us to thrive. Enter the sensorium!

Smell

Our sense of smell is primal. The capacity to smell is central to our survival and linked to our intelligence. In fact, scientists believe our brains evolved from the olfactory lobe. Smell alerts us to both danger and sustenance. For many animals, scent directs them to potential mates who have the DNA to ensure strong offspring. Even though we often mask our natural scent with deodorants and perfumes, our sense of smell is a superhero that bypasses conscious awareness to inform and protect us.

Body/Mindfulness: To wake up your sense of smell, close your eyes, put your palm to your nose, and take a good, long whiff. Not just a quick little snort, but a deep snuff. What do you smell? Without any judgment, without the why or the how, identify in two or three words what you smell, no matter how silly or strange it sounds. For example, when I smell my palm in this moment, I detect scents of sour, salty, and metal. What about you?

WRITE NOW! *For this writing invitation, you'll need a few jars of herbs and spices. Choose some you like and some you're not so crazy about. Let's start with one you like. Close your eyes and slowly inhale this herb or spice, allowing it to fill your senses. Be open to whatever memories, feelings, and sensations arise. Now, without naming the herb or spice, write down one word or phrase describing the scent. Not so easy, eh? It's challenging to name or describe a specific scent without naming what it is. Give it a try. Then do the same with an herb or spice you're not so fond of and follow the same process of describing it without naming it, if possible. For example, I could describe the scent of mint as refreshing, uplifting, effervescent, awakening, expansive, a summer day, a porch swing, or a cozy winter morning in front of the fireplace —* without ever having to say the word *mint.*

Examples

TURPENTINE by Karen Burt-Imira

> I am nine
> oil painting horses galloping

beneath star-ladled night sky.
Opening sharply to my deepest urge
throwing my head high
extending my rippling body
my legs beating out my own heart song
mane and tail whip-flashing wind.

MY GRANDMOTHER AT CHRISTMAS by Jeannie McKenzie

My grandmother's apron was crispy white
stiffened by explosions of flour
or the starch of her efficient ironing.

The grandmother
we saw only at Christmas
if we were lucky.

On arrival, her house a bouquet
of lavender hankies, mothballs,
Fels-Naptha soap.

Ceramic bowls
of golden sugar butter
vanilla and brandy.

Tempered by flour
sifted with Christmas spices
leavened with baking soda.

We stirred and slopped
the evolving goop into pans
with my grandmother's spatula.

Smoothing out the lumps
we'd then slide them into
her massive Wedgewood stove.

To alchemize
golden undertones
anise overtones,

my grandmother at Christmas.

Touch

Touch is our mother tongue. In our birth mother's wombs, we were encased and touched everywhere by the embryonic fluids in which we floated. Being squeezed through the birth canal is a full-body massage. One of the first sensations we feel when we're born is being caught or held in someone's hands, sometimes slapped to get us breathing. Before we even open our eyes, our tiny bodies know themselves through touch. Human and chimpanzee babies who are never touched rarely survive. How and whether we are touched as infants determines our health, both physical and emotional; our immune systems; and our relationships. We are social creatures who bond through touch. Our language is rich with touch and skin metaphors. We say a person gets under my skin, they rub me the wrong way, they make my skin crawl. Someone who is overly sensitive is touchy, and when something moves us deeply, it touches us. We are wired for touch.

Body/Mindfulness: Sit or lie down. Close your eyes and go inside. Allow your breath to flow in and out like tides. Use your dominant hand to try the three different kinds of touch, described below, on the skin of your opposite forearm. Try this with your eyes open and then with your eyes closed to discover which way allows you to sense more deeply. Notice what feelings, memories, images, sensations, and emotions arise in response to each different quality of touch. No judgment if you prefer one over the other; just notice and gather information to inform your writing.

Three Kinds of Touch

Feather: With the fingertips from one hand, caress your opposite forearm, using a light feathery touch. A tickle touch. Just notice, being aware of how it makes you feel. Try it with eyes open and eyes closed. Notice your experience. Do you receive or resist this quality of touch?

Fingernails: Use your fingernails on your opposite forearm, not hard enough to hurt but just enough to gently scratch. How do you respond to this quality of touch? Do you like it or not?

Palming: Use your palm, the whole inside of your hand, to rub your opposite forearm. How's this one for you? Do you find it soothing or stimulating? Do you like it or not?

WRITE NOW! *Write about your experience with these three different kinds of touch. Which one did you like the most, and which one the least? What feelings, images, memories, sensations, and emotions were evoked for you with each kind of touch? Go anywhere this takes you. It does not need to be logical or make* *sense. Keep trying the different kinds of touch to inform your writing. Be curious. Have fun.*

Examples

FEATHER TOUCH by Ann McGuire

Bu Bu Bu
          Butter

silky smooooooooth

ignites below the surface

fast
          frenetic
                    furies

          frequency flying
                    through nerve tendrils

the signal squeals
          from toes to top

a smile on my face

FINGERNAILS by Robyn Morgan

Scratch, scrape, needle
nail my coffin shut
I hold my breath
acidic vigilance
I am a watchdog

attack-ready
my teeth clenched
I retreat
trapped in my own skin
shut out from the delicious
depth of my erotic interior.
Sign posted:
DO NOT ENTER.

PALMING by Dawn Li

at the broken tip of my humerus
sewed up, one plate and eight screws
numb from shoulder to fingers
like a marshmallow
until you arrive
and touch me
with your palm
inch by inch
gently
   gently
      gently
bringing me
spring days
growing trees
budding flowers
rainforests

Sight

Sight is considered our dominant sense. Most of us depend on our eyesight more than any other sense, but do we really *see*?

Usually we just look and label. Tree, flower, sky, car, person. But what if we were to look at something as if seeing it for the first time? The late poet Allen Ginsberg, with whom I studied at Naropa University in summer 1996, talked about the concept of beginner's mind, or an attitude of openness. I would like to introduce the idea of beginner's *eyes.* Can we look with beginner's eyes and see what is there in front of us, with open presence and curiosity instead of labeling it, deciding we already know all about it, and moving on? Can we tune in to the essence of a thing and receive it, in its is-ness, as if meeting it for the first time? Let's practice beginner's eyes.

Body/Mindfulness: The best way I know to practice seeing with beginner's eyes is to first cleanse the eyes with darkness. For this, you'll need an eye mask, scarf, or blindfold, something to cover your eyes and block out the light. We want to immerse our eyes in darkness. Put the blindfold on and allow yourself to relax, sink in, and receive the darkness into your eyes. Open your eyes under the blindfold and look into the dark, letting it relax your eyes and cleanse your vision. Stay with this experience for a few moments. Then take the blindfold off, slowly opening your eyes to a soft focus. What I mean by soft focus is letting your eyes and vision be slightly unfocused, almost sleepy, resting gently wherever they land. Allow yourself to simply see, without naming, labeling, or classifying the visual information — just taking in shape, size, color, texture, proximity. Be open to the relationships between form and space. Notice what it feels like to look with beginner's eyes. It can feel like we're seeing with our whole being.

WRITE NOW!   *For this writing invitation you'll need a fruit or vegetable. Go get one now and come right back. Look at your*

fruit or veggie with beginner's eyes, as if you're from another
planet, seeing it for the very first time. Write some words or phrases
that come to mind. Consider shape, size, texture, color. What is
rare and unique, beautiful and strange, memorable and inspiring
about this fruit or vegetable? Describe it using your beginner's eyes.

Examples

D'ANJOU PEAR by Nicole Phillips

> Your skin gleams
> wet red maple leaves
> laid leathery against
> shadowed stone.
> Golden watercolors
> painted down
> your curves
> your plump
> oval-egg body
> rippling.
>
> When I spin your ribbed
> tree-stump stem
> I see the scabs
> from cuts you've healed
> dark-brown dry dimples.
>
> I rip off the plastic sticker
> always takes a piece
> of your precious kiln-fired skin
> and sink my teeth into your flesh
> opening your voluptuous
> creamy, juicy rump
> that massages my gums

gushes over my lips
dissolves on my tongue.
Mama earth made
pudding inside you.

TEMPTRESS by Mary Pritchard

Ah, fruit of Eden
fruit of Paradise

Temptress
blushing red

Plucked gently
from your tree

I hold your cool smooth
roundness in my hand

Feeling the stem
that clings to life

Inhaling your fresh sweetness
yearning for the first bite

Juice dribbling
down my chin

Your mystery
within a star

Cradling your seeds
as new life awaits.

Hearing

Hearing and listening are acts of deep receiving we perform with our whole being. Is there a difference between hearing and listening? Hearing is about registering the sounds around us. Notice the sounds you hear around you right now. We can easily tune them in or block them out, the refrigerator, the air conditioner, birds chirping, insects buzzing, kids yelling, a car horn blowing. We're bathed in sound. We orient by sound. Without sight, we can get around by connecting through our sense of hearing, but without hearing, we can feel isolated. We've always been in touch with sound, from the beginning of our lives in utero, when we were rocked to the lullaby of our mother's heartbeat, *ba-bum, ba-bum*. Unless we were born hearing-challenged, the landscape of sound is as natural to us as breathing. Then there's listening, the deeper level of hearing. It's about giving our full attention to the sounds we hear. It means getting quiet enough that we consciously absorb and digest the information we're hearing. Let's explore hearing and listening.

Body/Mindfulness: Sit or lie down. Get comfy. Settle in and relax. Close your eyes and allow your breath to breathe you, in and out. Get quiet and deepen into your sense of hearing. It's like opening a gate to your whole body. Tune in to the sounds around you — birds, dogs, children, cars, airplanes, construction, music — and take it all in, really listening. Follow one sound, and see where it takes you in terms of feeling, thought, sensation, memory.

WRITE NOW! *You'll need a few different pieces of music for this writing invitation. In my workshops, I use a variety such as*

Native American flute, opera, whale song, Tuvan throat singing, Tibetan bowls, a chorus of crickets. Choose whatever you like. Listen on headphones if possible. Play each piece for a few minutes, allowing yourself to respond in mind-spill or stream-of-consciousness writing to the sounds you hear. Then take any of the words or phrases from your writing and arrange them into a poem. See if you can find a way to make the words on your page mirror the sounds and rhythms you heard.

Examples

WHALE SONG by Ann McGuire

    I am sucked

    D
     O
      W
       N

    in

    D
     A
      R
      K

    green ink

    M O U M B A

    shadow couriers
    shift & dive

OWAMII

I don't understand

but I want
to follow
their elusive
beauty.

TUCSON DESERT by Karen Burt-Imira

Echoes from the canyon edge
          over the tall gestures of saguaros
I holler out and the wind hollers back
          brash and haunting
I sing out and the sky sings back
          calling to me by the name of my tones
Our songs meet midair and fly among the ocotillos
          waving coral crimson hands
I warble. I croon. I cry out rhythmic notes and syllables
          gushing from deep inner canyons
A flash flood thrown into the wash of the wind
          carried back around to me
I'm hawk dancing her red tail
          through high echoing melodies.

Taste

We have been feasting on smell, touch, sight, and hearing, and now let's turn to the true feast, taste! Food is what author Diane Ackerman, in *A Natural History of the Senses*, calls our "social sense." In every kind of celebration or gathering the world over, whether for an evening dinner, a marriage ceremony, or a wake, we eat together. Cooking and eating are ceremonies of survival, which used to include hunting and celebrating a kill and then dividing the bounty among the tribe. It's rare for people to eat alone. Yet these days so many of us live alone and lead such busy lives, we find ourselves grabbing lunch on the go, throwing a prepared meal into the microwave, plopping down in front of the TV to unwind from the day with a bag of chips or a pint of ice cream. Food becomes a way to fill the void. We learn early on to equate food with love. As infants we were given a breast or a bottle to quell our crying, so we learn to comfort ourselves by eating as we try to fill the emptiness that is deeper than hunger. Taste, like touch, is woven into our language. When we love someone, we call them our sweetie, sugar, honey, sugarplum, honeybun. When a relationship ends badly, we say it turned sour. When someone has lost at love or life and holds a grudge, we say they're bitter. When someone is exciting, passionate, and perhaps unpredictable, we dub them spicy. And a good, capable, dependable person is worth their salt; they are the salt of the earth. Let's do some tasting.

Five Tastes

> **Sweet:** fruit, dessert, candy
> **Sour:** lemon, cheese, vinegar
> **Salty:** chips, salted nuts, umeboshi plum
> **Spicy:** salsa, chilies, Dijon mustard
> **Bitter:** dark chocolate, arugula, coffee

Body/Mindfulness: For this one you'll need some food items, like the ones suggested above, to represent each flavor.

You won't need more than a bite of each. Get ready for some hands-on, lip-licking fun!

WRITE NOW! *Set up your taste samples, and write from one of the two approaches described below.*

> **Full-immersion writing:** Spend sixty seconds with each taste. Choose the one that is most alive or evocative for you, and write for fifteen minutes about where that taste takes you in terms of feelings, ideas, images, sensations, memories. You can challenge yourself further by writing without naming the flavor, by not saying "lemon" or "sour," for example, but just the images or feelings that arise.

> **Mind-spill writing:** Spend three minutes with each flavor, tasting and writing about each, one after another, for a total of fifteen minutes. Put your pen to paper, and write anything and everything that comes to mind as you taste each flavor. You can challenge yourself further by writing without naming the flavor, not saying "nuts" or "salty," for example, but just the images and feelings that arise.

Examples

SWEET by Jeannie McKenzie

> Plump earthy roundness
> this season's first
> watermelon.

One crisp bite
flows a river
stickyseedspittingslurp
summer sunshine.

They stripped your seeds
like declawing a cat
more space
for your sweetness.

Your old-school crunch
left behind
our sugar-toothed desire
marching us back
to the never enough
of mother's milk.

SOUR by Nicole Phillips

Sour grass
sour lemon
pucker me up
sourpuss
until all my
everything
contracts
and I don't
even recognize
myself
in the mirror.

QUEEN OF THE CHESAPEAKE by Helen Baxt

Greetings to you, tangy siren of summer
with zest you emphatically announce your return

delighted by our long-awaited reunion
as our tribal gathering celebrates your arrival.

Boat horns bellow, a salty breeze cools the air
seagulls laugh, feverishly mimicking each other's songs
wafts of vinegar, the wine of the fish, tickles my nose
I twinge and squint from the painful jab of your sensual
    bite.

The rare if not only occasion when a tart beer joins my
    lips
piled on yesterday's news or strips of hearty brown paper
mallets furiously bang, eager to seize the sweet lump of
    backfin
but you're the real star of this native feast.
The food of my homeland smothered in your fiery coat
I relish in your return, though we are rarely without you
there have been impostors, but none can compete —
you, the legendary, proud and audacious,
Queen of the Chesapeake.

SPICY by Dawn Li

    haa haa haa

    from the tip
    of my tongue

    to the button
    of my belly

    haa haa haa
    burning

to the flame
of summer

steaming
me clean

as the sun.

BITTERSWEET CACAO by Nicole Phillips

We met Lana at the Luna Lodge
on the Osa Peninsula, Costa Rica.

She offered us dark-brown cacao beans
and nibs, bitter earth bites
of pain and pleasure.
Their strength makes me want to sprout thick hair
their vitality accelerates my mind
their love opens my heart.

We prayed together each day
for abundance and protection
while we drank ground cacao beans
in hot creamy coconut milk
with spicy ginger and sweet cinnamon.

Poured as an offering
into the thirsty soil
and our eager mouths.

CHAPTER 5

Wild Heart

Cultivate the courage to be true to your wild heart.

What does *wild* mean to you? Does it mean reckless, crazy, out of control? Does it conjure images of old-growth forests, rivers clean enough to drink from, healthy biomes, and perhaps humans — living in harmonious relationship with each other and the planet, before we were conditioned to take more than we need, out of fear and scarcity, competition and greed? When I speak of *wild*, I am pointing to living from our truth, our original, essential, instinctive nature, uncolonized and uncompromised by civilization and mores; I'm talking about living from our wild hearts. How do we find our wild? How do we return to and kindle our true? For many of us it takes a major life event such as loss, injury, illness, or trauma to make us question everything we've ever been taught and catapult us into a completely new way of being — a wilder way, one closer to our true natures. These kinds of major life events invite us to take stock and evaluate our lives, asking the necessary question: Are we living true to our hearts? This is a deep dive into asking yourself, Am I happy, am I fulfilled, am I passionate about my life, am I living my potential, am I fulfilling my purpose, am I contributing to the world in ways I find meaningful? And if not, am

I willing to change? It is an opportunity for a life reimagined, redefined, reinvented.

Start by asking yourself some of these questions, being open, truthful, and nonjudgmental about what answers arise, and then we'll dig in together.

- How's your energy, your vitality?
- Are you in tune with yourself?
- Where are you on the barometer of balance?
- Are you doing work you love, work that engages your values and your passion?
- How are your relationships? Are they reciprocal, fulfilling, inspiring? Do they meet you at your growing edge?
- Do you find your life exciting, fulfilling, challenging, nourishing?
- Are you growing in all the ways that matter to you?
- Do you contribute your talents and skills to help others in meaningful ways?
- Are you waging love for what you value and treasure in this life?

Waking Your Wild

If your wild nature were a sleeping animal that just woke up, what would it do naturally? How would it move? How would it meet its needs? How does it know what it wants? A part of each of us knows exactly what we need and want, but we often push away this knowing. We feel the call to stretch or dance, move somewhere new, start a new job, try a new hobby, leave a relationship, start dating again, but we squelch the call and remain small, comfortable, secure. When we don't ask ourselves and others for what we truly want and need, eventually we stop hearing the call altogether. We distance ourselves from our deepest knowing, and we abandon our truth. We fall out of touch with our vitality and forget who we truly are. Then we wonder why we're sick, depressed, angry, addicted, unfulfilled, empty, numb, lost. Let's dive deep and open our hearts to the wild calling, our innate knowing of how to be true to ourselves.

Body/Mindfulness: Sit or lie down, close your eyes, and settle in. Allow your breath to find you, filling and emptying you in tides. Feel yourself supported by what's underneath and behind you as you let your body soften and open. Make yourself at home in your vast inner world. Say hello. Imagine what it would feel like and who you would be if you allowed your inner wild woman to come out and play. You know her, the one who remembers that your life is a gift, the one who makes you feel a little scared and a lot excited and free. The one who finds joy in everyday life, who knows how to turn the ordinary into the extraordinary, who knows her mind and doesn't take any bullshit. The one who stays true to herself no matter what others think or say. The one who welcomes her own special weirdness. The one with her own style, who makes her own way, who says what she thinks, who doesn't compromise out of fear or need but fiercely, bravely, passionately, wildly makes room for herself in the world. Invite this wild one to come out and play!

WRITE NOW! *Write all the wild and wonderful things that come to mind when you give yourself permission to be fully you. This is your chance to explore who you truly are and what your life looks like when there is no one around to tell you otherwise.*

Who would you be and how would you live if you were completely true to your heart? How would you build a life based on what you find most inspiring and fulfilling? What makes you feel deeply and wildly alive? Give yourself permission to explore. You might start with a phrase such as My wild woman ... *and then tell us all about her!*

Examples

MY WILD WOMAN by Karen Burt-Imira

My wild woman had many ideas of wild
she chased them with determined desperation.
Now only one image comes to guide her —
vibrations of silent growing grass.
My wild woman pillaged her years
tearing open rules, stomping on stigmas
foraging for new foods of life.
Now she ponders, harvesting visions
from the darkest womb
humming with creation.

My wild woman threw herself
voraciously at life
she consumed moonlit passions
danced and made love on black sand
where the jungle meets the sea.
Now she tastes the essence
that illuminates the shores
of her inhale and exhale.

My wild woman trekked
and tangoed with a myriad

of tamed and untamed
loveless lovers.
Now she knows one peaceful galaxy
of togetherness, mutual
unconditional devotees.

My wild woman birthed her children ecstatically
she was one of her own midwives.
Now she points herself all day, every day
toward a portal of vibrant stillness
pregnant with everything.

My wild woman made every mistake
she gloried triumphant, paid bitter dues
learned the hard way.
Now she treads lightly upon the earth
whispering her prayers for freedom and joy
and to be ordinary,
ordained into the Simple Order of All Life,
a priestess of the Silent Growing Grass.

WOMANIFESTO by Nicole Phillips

My wild woman wears leather
tanned in sun
from elk she has hunted.
She cuts through, she cuts in
she lives outside
sleeps roofless under stars.
She stops looking in mirrors
her hair becomes a bushel
of cones and flowers.
She gets lost in canyonlands

when it's 99 degrees
diverges from water.

Covered in mud and horsefly bites
she surrenders her body
to red stone slabs.
Goes into a dream delirium
has a vision of an eagle
that guides her back home.
My wild woman knows plant medicine
by smell, touch, and taste
she heals herself and others.
She sits in a teepee, women only,
to bleed moony, while men tend the fire outside
serve up grilled meat and raspberry leaf tea.
My wild woman feels lost
mornings and afternoons
without her own human baby.

Come dusk, she finds herself
in cherry sage flowers
her grief marinating her dreams.

Holy Compost

Let's return to the soil, and to compost specifically. Compost is a truly amazing phenomenon. Compost is alchemy. How amazing to put organic matter into the soil so that micro-organisms feast on it, turning it into rich humus from which new life sprouts. Compost is a metaphor we can live by. We can bury our old, outdated modes of behavior and renew our energy. When I talk about burying stuff, I don't mean throwing it away or hiding it but putting it back into the soil of our psyches to be turned by our own awareness into compost from which new growth emerges. When we become aware of the thought patterns and behaviors that limit, deplete, and drain our life force, we can choose to give that energy back to our metaphorical soil. Then we allow compost to do its magic, to turn the old into the new. And we begin to dream into what we'd like to plant and grow.

Body/Mindfulness: Close your eyes. Get comfy. Allow your body to soften and melt open so you can access your inner world. Place a hand on your heart and a hand on your belly to help you focus and ground. Ask yourself what you do or think that limits and drains your energy, and be willing to receive the answer. Then ask yourself if you're willing to let go of these limiting things and let compost have its way with them. What new ways of being might you plant and grow in the new soil made from the compost of the old? Listen for the answers. Say thank you to whatever arises.

WRITE NOW! *Make a list of all the things you do that no longer serve you. Dive in as deep or as shallow as you like. Bury the tight jeans along with the rage at your mother. Throw out the too much time spent on Facebook, along with the ex who cheated on you. The psyche doesn't know the difference. It just knows these things hurt and drain your energy. So what are you ready to let go of? Write that list. Now make a list of all the things that help you feel happy, calm, energized, inspired, productive, balanced, and fulfilled. Arrange these two lists side by side so you can see how they echo each other. Make connections between what you choose to compost and what you choose to grow anew. Be willing to get down and dirty, and turn that compost!*

Examples

FACADES by Mary Pritchard

> I bury my facade of Happy Mary Sunshine
> when grief, sorrow, and loss
> lurk beneath the surface.
>
> I plant my heart broken open
> freeing my pain and love and tears
> inviting others to join me in my truth.
>
> I bury my facade of inadequacy,
> always falling short,
> never enough.
>
> I plant joyful, beautiful imperfection
> willing vulnerability,
> courage, and faith in myself.
>
> I bury scorn for my body
> critical voices inside me and around me
> my need to shrink into the background.
>
> I plant love of this beautiful body
> the gift of every inch, every pound, every bulge
> I plant pride standing tall.
>
> I plant short-sleeved shirts exposing flabby arms
> that give world-class hugs
> cherished by all who receive them.
>
> I plant myself
> perfectly imperfect
> wild open heart.

COMPOST by Jeannie McKenzie

I compost judgment of my decaying form
transmutation of smooth soft skin
into dry wrinkled bark.
I propagate acceptance
of my ever-changing body.

I dig deep into the soil of my grief
through worms and decay and broken eggshells
in search of the season of letting go
so I can erupt
in unfettered expansion
and fully blossom.

I dig in the humus
pull out the sticks of unworthiness
chopping them down
into bits of enough,
enough is enough is enough!

I ready myself for new roots
I myceliate into interconnectedness
companion plants of worthy and beautiful
thrive in unexpected
inexplicable wonder,
a harvest of wholeness.

Atonement

When I lived on the Big Island of Hawaii, I learned about
the practice of ho'oponopono, the Hawaiian wisdom way
for making things right with ourselves and others. The word

ho'oponopono comes from *ho'o*, "to make," and *pono*, "right." The repetition of the word *pono* means "doubly right" or being right with self and others. It boils down to apology, forgiveness, gratitude, and love. Once you get the hang of it, you realize these are the only phrases we ever really need to communicate to ourselves and others: *I'm sorry, please forgive me, thank you, I love you.* The healing that comes from these four simple phrases is profound. You can write or say them to yourself or to someone else. I have written copious pages of these to people with whom I have an unresolved issue, and I'll tell you the most amazing thing: after writing these phrases to someone, though I haven't reached out and shared what I've written, I often hear from them within a few days, out of the blue, even if we haven't spoken in years. They work! You can practice them again and again, as healing happens layer by layer. Let's give it a try.

Ho'oponopono has four parts:

Apology: I'm sorry.
Forgiveness: Please forgive me. / I forgive you.
Gratitude: Thank you.
Love: I love you.

Body/Mindfulness: Close your eyes and sink in. Say hello to the companionship of your breath. Place a hand on your heart and a hand on your belly. Arrive in yourself. Say each of the ho'oponopono phrases to yourself one at a time, noticing any feelings, sensations, or memories that arise. *I'm sorry, please forgive me, thank you, I love you.* In my experience, when I say each phrase, whatever needs healing rises to the surface of its own accord. I keep saying the phrases to myself either silently or aloud, until the hurt feels met, resolved, and released and I feel lighter and at peace. You can also approach this by asking if there's something you condemn in yourself, something you're punishing yourself for, holding against yourself, and asking what needs your apology, forgiveness, gratitude, appreciation. Try saying the phrases privately to yourself while directing them to someone with whom you have unresolved issues. Stay with each phrase long enough for it to do its healing work. You will feel when the energy shifts and releases. You may feel lighter, cleansed, peaceful, free, and you may find that your tears come.

WRITE NOW! *Take time with each of the four ho'oponopono phrases and address them to yourself. Write down everything you want to apologize to yourself for: I'm sorry for… Everything you want to forgive yourself for: I forgive you for… Everything you feel gratitude for in yourself: thank you for… And everything you love in yourself: I love you for… After you write these to yourself, you can write them to anyone else in your life who might need to hear any or all of these words from you. Even if you don't share it with the person you wrote it to, working with these phrases creates ripples of healing in the fabric of the universe. It shifts things. It's potent. You and the other person will feel it.*

Examples

I'M SORRY & THANK YOU by Liz Kughn

> I'm sorry the journey was long and arduous
> and many times, I made you go without food and water.

> I'm sorry I insisted that you be perfect and I'm sorry for
>   my never-ending criticism
> always wanting you to be a thinner, stronger, better
>   version of yourself.

I forgive you for being afraid and ashamed of so many
    things
and for not understanding social media and forgetting
    how to make salmon.

I thank you for admitting when you need help
though this feels at times like a threat to your very
    existence.

I thank you for being angry and messy
even when it seems to make people uncomfortable.

I thank you for waking up and walking through the pain
when most parts of you want to run.

I love you through your disorder, your piles on the floor
and too many glasses of wine.

I love your lemon cake on Monday afternoon
even when your jeans are too tight.

I love your passionate confusion about parenting
and not ever really knowing if you're doing the right
    thing.

I love your tender tears as you hand her the money,
her sign saying she has three children and no food.

I FORGIVE YOU by Geneva Toland

Come now, my love,
we are finished
with the long crawl of repenting

scraped knees, wet cheeks, and hot eyes
you have done enough.

Yes, I was angry
yes, I had every right to be
yes, there was a long time
that you wouldn't listen.

But then you did,
and you sat with me
and held my hurt
you told me all the things necessary
to heal a heart like mine —

I believe you. You are right.
It's not your fault.
You didn't deserve it.
I'm sorry.
Again and again
through darkness and sleet,
snowfalls and summer rain
you gave me space
to be bold in my bitter.

Thank you for your attentive
apology, but spring is here
to transform and transfix,
the seeds of what is ahead
are waiting, ready
for our fertile rain.

Let us dance in the storm clouds
let us shed the past

open our mouths, wide
to the sky.

It is time, sweet love.
I forgive you.

SOME LOVE by Shontae T.

I'm sorry for avoiding you, not loving you,
putting you on the back burner
for so long.

I forgive us for not knowing how to nurture both sides,
for the lack of understanding ourselves,
and for trying to ignore us as a whole.

Thank you for coming back for the other part of we,
the parts that appreciate and cultivate our needs,
and for unlocking us with our key.

I love you for all that you are, and all that you ain't.
I love us, I love we, I love you, myself,
and I finally love me.

I LOVE MYSELF by Ani Meier

How many times did I say this, half meaning it?
How many times did I say this, as I locked eyes
with the woman in the glass, wondering,
"So does some magic fairy bless me now?"

I've been holding her gaze every other day
in the dark wood frame, blessed by flowers,

painted at the edges after the wreckage of Ida,
and I think, "She has never looked better."

I woke the next day fetching light like wind,
receiving her clear direction, and there we were
three friends at the pawpaw sanctuary,
where Maryland, Delaware, and Pennsylvania meet,
picking through hickory nuts and drinking roasted
    herbal coffee
like it was any other day at the end of summer.

I love myself, so I ate every fig
and pawpaw offered me,
a feast for these two eyes.
I love myself, so I let myself receive all
the kindness growing around me,
like sprawling dandelion and chickweed.
I love myself, so I swung from the tallest tree
in the richest woodland
beneath the brightest full moon.

Belonging

Belonging is one of our most primal needs. After food, shelter, and safety, we seek belonging. And though we long to be included by others, and being part of the tribe is essential, first we must belong to ourselves. Let's explore who and what helped shape our early sense of belonging, what experiences, activities, people, and feelings created our sense of identity. Then let's challenge these things and ask ourselves if our identity aligns with our wild heart, which thrives on growth, passion, sovereignty, and freedom. Are we living true to ourselves, or do we follow the norms, compromise to be accepted, to feel like we belong?

Body/Mindfulness: Close your eyes. Lean back. Settle in. Allow your breath to breathe you. No need to change or fix it. Simply make contact and say hello to whatever rhythm or texture your breath shows up in right now. Place a hand on your heart and a hand on your belly and tune in with yourself. Say the words *I belong* a few times to yourself, quietly or aloud. Notice what feelings and images arise. Ask yourself to whom and what you belong and why. Does this sense of belonging feel true to you? Perhaps some of the people and things to which you belong feel true, and perhaps some don't. Which ones ring true? Notice if you've made any compromises in order to belong.

WRITE NOW! *Start by writing the words* I belong to ... *Then look through the categories below and write anything and everything that comes to mind. Don't judge. Don't argue with yourself. Simply say yes to what arises, and write it down. You can always ditch what you don't want or need later. Give yourself plenty of ideas to work with. Be true to what you hear in yourself. Give yourself space and permission to explore. Then pick out the strongest and juiciest lines, and arrange them into a piece of writing you like.*

Categories of Belonging

Activities
Best or worst experiences and memories
City, town, country
Clothing

Community
Creative projects
Equipment (such as your bike, camera, swim fins, back-
    pack, skis, car, phone)
Feelings, emotions, attitudes, beliefs
Food and cooking
Good and bad habits
Hobbies
Home and furnishings
Nature areas, sacred spots, favorite places
People: family, children, parents, partners, friends,
    business associates
Work and service

Examples

I BELONG by Michèle Coppin

> I belong to low gray skies
> to the sound of rain on cobblestones
> to the North Sea
> to tides
> to wind
> to confessing on Wednesdays
> so pale in my navy-blue uniform.
>
> I belong to the blinding sun
> my shadow dark and purple
> to palettes of peeling walls
> to the blood of bulls
> to bloody crowns of thorns
> on pallid wooden foreheads
> to shots of amber mezcal.

I belong to the North
to the cold
the silent sound of snow
to so many trees
dark
whispering
spirits
to black skies
dancing lights
to the call of loons
to the howling solitude of storms.

Not really belonging,
just visiting, thank you.

I BELONG by Nicole Phillips

I belong to bare feet and ancient spirits dancing.
I belong to rhythm. To the drum, to heartbeats and
    birdsong.
I belong to Paula's farm, jumping in hay bales, milking
    goats, swimming in the pond.
I belong to tear elixirs, sourced from the well of my heart
    to integrate all my feelings.
I belong to strawberries, figs, and pluots. Wisteria,
    lupine, and wild sweet peas.
I belong to long walks. To flowers. To colors.
I belong to olive skin, moon craters, moonshine, and a
    dark invisible side.
I belong to ginger tea, peppermint oil, and homemade
    salve.
I belong to singing to heal the wound of keeping quiet.

I belong to Boulder Creek, Eldorado Canyon, the Yuba River, Tennessee Valley Beach.
I belong to words woven, songs springing. I belong.

The Whole Shebang!

What if when you applied for a job or created an online profile, instead of the regular points of education, employment, athletic prowess, creative hobbies, community service, and all the other mad skills that show how you shine, you wrote a more poetic bio that reflected your unique and wild genius? You in?!

Body/Mindfulness: Close your eyes, settle in, and imagine you're stepping right into your true wild-woman self. Inhabit and become her. You know you want to. You know she's been waiting your whole life for you to choose her. Absorb her passion and her purpose. Imbibe her permission to be herself, unapologetically. Let her sing and shine through you. What does it feel like to be her, see the world through her eyes, move through her body, speak out from her voice? Towanda!

WRITE NOW! *Write a poetic bio that expresses your wild she-heart. Give yourself permission to not care what anyone else thinks of you. Write about what makes you you, as though you were attracting your dream mate, dream job, dream life. All the special things that make you who you are matter. They're vital, and they work in your favor. Like the fact that you prefer to walk barefoot, that you write love letters to people you don't know, talk to ghosts, talk to trees, put a shot of whiskey in your morning coffee, always wear hot-pink panties, reveal your deepest secrets to strangers on* *the plane, spend one weekend a month eating coffee ice cream in bed while watching old movies, or that you're seriously considering packing up shop and going to work with endangered animals in the Galapagos. Or that you're writing a book. Or that you're moving to New Zealand to be with someone you met online. Be yourself. Be your wild, wonderful self. No one to impress. No one to disappoint. What makes you feel alive? Left to your own devices, how do you choose to live and love?*

Examples

SHE by Helen Baxt

> Born of the Lion in Southern California
> she entered the world with a mighty roar
> gifted a loving family, not flesh of her flesh
> but of one heart and belonging.
>
> She sings to the sun and dances with the moon
> she's the sway of reeds in the breeze
> and the beat of a steady drum
> a seagull's song on a sun-drenched beach
> the melody on the tip of your tongue.
>
> She's the words in her shadow book
> the drip of her intention candle
> decorated in scars of chaos
> and bruises worn with dignity.
>
> She's familiar with loss and pain
> wild love and rousing joy.
> She's been stolen and owned
> shared and granted

bought and sold.
Her strength is born of surrender
her beauty from decay.

She is at her best when
draped in vulnerability
tangled yet unraveled
born again and again
from her humble fervent heart
wrapped with an untidy bow.

MOON DANCER by Nicole Phillips

She is a wild whimsical warrior
a wily witch
a white jasmine flower.
She's long and strong
with hips swinging free
long legs, long before human.

She's a mirthy word wizard, whirling
a nomadic seamstress
threading our wounds
with illimitable love.
She touches many with her spirit
bathing in lavender tears
dancing silver
under a glistening moon.

CHAPTER 6

Sanctuary

Create inner peace in a crazy world.

Most of us can agree that the world is one crazy place to live in these days, and yet it's home. So while we can't always change the chaos outside us, we can create sanctuary within. Writing is one of the best ways I know to do this. Writing provides a refuge in which we can pause, commune with deep self, and nourish ourselves back into equanimity. My other favorite way to find peace in this wacky world is through spending time in nature. When we attune with nature we recalibrate to earth's rhythms, connect with our ancient ancestry of soil and stars, and remember ourselves as part of the great mystery. Join me now as we make safe sanctuary and touch the still point in this whirling-dervish world.

Ancestry

Who are we? Where do we come from? How did we get here? What is our ancestry? And by ancestry I mean more than just our parents, grandparents, great-grandparents, and so on. I mean how we are connected to the ancient molecules of life. We have atoms in our bodies that are 13 billion years old, birthed in the heart fire of stars and in the belly of

114

water droplets. We contain bits of all life-forms. What do we share with dinosaurs and dragonflies and dirt? With ferns and ginkgo trees and bristlecone pines? There are saltwater oceans in our blood and tears, and stardust in our skin. Our root system feeds on everything that has returned its body to the earth. What's your ancestry? Where do you come from? What are you made of? What bits of ancient life are singing through you?

Body/Mindfulness: Close your beautiful eyes and settle in. Make yourself comfy. Feel the places where your body meets what's underneath and behind you, allowing you to feel supported as you soften and melt open. Feel your breath breathing you in waves. Relax into the vast cosmos of your inner being. Say hello to the swirling, pulsing energy that is you, that is the universe. Feel how your energy is connected to the whole matrix of life. As you breathe in and out, imagine the breath of all life breathing through you, as you. Stay with this feeling of interconnectedness as you allow ideas and images to come to you about who you are, what you're made of, where you come from.

WRITE NOW! *Write all the ideas and images that come to mind as you explore the bigger picture of your ancestry, asking yourself: Where am I from, what am I made of, what ancient and current life is breathing and beating through me right now? Dig down deep. Reach far and wide. Acknowledge the stars and the soil that live in your wild bones. Write about the oceans in your blood, the lightning in your marrow, the jungle monkeys swinging in your limbs, the whales singing up your dreamtime. Life is one big organism, and we are part of it. Anything goes. Have fun!*

Examples

ANCESTRY by Jeannie McKenzie

> I am a wanderer
> dropped from the heart
> of the universe.
>
> I caught a ride on a shooting star
> through timeless time
> welcomed by my newest mother,
> the earth. She sprouted me
> through mycelial roots
> into the lineage of trees.
>
> Swimming on the edge of a whale's fin
> I was baptized in her oceanic waters
> I caught photons till I was dizzy
> and became my own descendant.
>
> A fire-breathing, wide-winged dragon
> soaring wise and wondrous,
> I was introduced to my grandparents
> the Elements
> and next of kin, the elephants
> pounding rhythms through savannas.
>
> Heartbeats of history
> in search of water,
> I evaporated into a cloud
> I surveyed all my relations
> from the expanse above.

Then, shaken loose
in a thunderstruck moment,
I tumbled
      into
         free fall
into the embrace of gravity
granite, clay, fossil, forest
mountainous arms
of my magnificent mother.

She swirled and twirled me
through DNA strands
photosynthesized and composted me
washed and burned me
then bathed me in the tides
of her salty blood.

I transformed over and over
through dark veils of fear
yearning to return to the light
and with every turn,
deeper into compassion.

MY ANCESTRY by Karen Burt-Imira

I was a newborn star
spun out from the heavenly yoni
of a traveling black hole.

I rode the blacksmithing winds
who forged my glowing form
into a womanly earthbody
and cooled me in the river of time.

Infused with timeless purpose
I joined the wild equine nation
and watched over them.

Their streaming manes
braided into my own
as I rode the electric energy
pouring from their backs.

Everything Contains Everything

Let's explore this interconnected web of life. Ever notice how everything is not only connected to everything else but is also contained within everything else? Everything has a little bit of everything within it. In his book *Peace Is Every Step*, the late Vietnamese Zen Buddhist teacher Thich Nhat Hanh addressed this by writing about a cloud floating in a sheet of paper, bringing our attention to how the clouds made the rain that grew the trees that were cut down and made into paper. Life is a web of interbeing. Everything contains everything. And we are part of it. By naming the parts and finding the connections, we weave ourselves back into wholeness and belonging, into interbeing.

Body/Mindfulness: Close your eyes and settle in. Ride the waves of your breath. Invite your body to relax and open so that what's inside you becomes accessible. Choose something, anything, really, like a pillow or a pen, a table or a coffee mug, a guitar or a dress, and follow it through until you have a sense of all the elements contained within it and how they are related, like in Thich Nhat Hanh's poem.

WRITE NOW! *Write the life story of your chosen object, including as much as possible about what it contains and the process it has gone through to become what it is. Look for the interdependent relationships between the elements that comprise your object, like rain clouds providing water so that trees can grow and be cut down to make paper. You have permission to be inventive. This doesn't need to be scientific or factual. Use your imagination to make connections. The whole universe is contained within each part. Perhaps include even yourself!*

Examples

BLUE BOWL by Meredith Heller

> This blue bowl
> like an empty sky
> turned inside out
> with small fractures
> where its earthen soul shows through
> where its shine has been rubbed away
> by stars passing through.
>
> This blue bowl
> turned on a wheel
> turned in someone's hands
> born of the thick brown clay
> that lay asleep inside the earth
> holding her bones together.
>
> This blue bowl
> glazed with cerulean-blue paint
> from glass that tumbled
> onto a tiny beach

in the Greek Islands
by the Mediterranean Sea
where one day, when I was seventeen,
I saw a man catch an octopus with his bare hands
and beat it against a rock until it was dead
and then take it home and cook it up
with garlic and onions,
leeks and tomatoes from his garden
and feed it to his wife and children
after a long day
making blue glaze in the hot sun.

This blue bowl
fired in the kiln
with fire from the sun
or wherever fire comes from.
Where does fire live before it's born?
Does the spark that makes fire
come from the stars
that circle the sky
that live inside my bowl?

This blue bowl
which I now hold in my hands
and pass into the hands of my lover
who sits beside me munching
popcorn and peanuts
and small pieces of dark chocolate
that he feeds me
from this blue bowl
with his fingers laughing
his mouth smiling
his eyes like river rocks, shining.

This blue bowl
held in the hands of everyone
who helped make it
and bring it to market
where I saw it and loved it
bought it and carried it home
in the basket on my bike.

This blue bowl
like an empty sky
but not so empty
so, so full
of all the lives that helped
shape this vessel
which now holds its own
open palms
up to the light.

THE TABLE by Heather Irene Bush

In my fourteen-year-old bedroom,
I kept a wobbly table
next to my waterbed.

The top surface was shaped like a stop sign.
It was rickety, but it had a door.
That's where I kept my private words
and my secret stash of Marlboro Reds.

If you wanna know the truth,
cigarettes make me woozy,
but they sure as hell help the words come.

The words were mine alone.
They inhabited the diaries I kept

and could read straight through in a single day.
Diaries filled with Kurt Cobain suicide poems
and other trauma I had not yet learned to discern.

And there were letters in the table.
Letters from John, a nineteen-year-old artist
I had met at a Christian coffee shop
my aunt once took me to in Highland, Indiana.

John,
whose name, though biblical,
was forbidden.
But I loved him
and corresponded with him
through most of my teenage years.

When I left my parents' house,
I emptied the table
and carried about a hundred of his letters
in the various suitcases I hauled all around the world.

The table was moved to the bathroom.
No longer a sanctuary to keep my sacred scripture,
it was used to house toilet paper for about twenty years.

My mom even kept a Daily Word calendar on the top
so you could reflect on some Christianity
while you used the bathroom.

Now I'm forty-one years old.
And somehow I got that little four-legged table back.
My father refinished it, and he even fixed the wobble.

It stands sturdy in my living room
with a translucent blue lamp from Marshall's on top.
Only now, there's nothing inside.

I used to keep an old Christmas cookie tin
filled with my weed stash,
but last winter, I got a bout of vertigo that lasted four weeks
and I suspect it was the weed that triggered it.

So I gave the whole cookie tin, weed, pipes,
papers and all to my ex-boyfriend.
No questions asked.

MY THUMBNAIL by Jeannie McKenzie

I'll start with my left thumbnail
not smooth and painted
but three waves on one side
and a series of dashes on the other.

In Chinese medicine nails reflect the liver
smooth nails mean a smooth life —
that's not what's going on here.

Anger started early in me
because I was born a girl
and that's not what my mother wanted.

I fought her for trying to make me
be the right kind of girl
who wears the right kind of dresses
and has the right kind of manners
and doesn't talk back.

Swallowing anger with lima beans for dinner
all of them must be eaten for the poor starving children
on the other side of the world or no cinnamon-toast
     breakfast.

Stubbornness set in at an early age
the way to be angry in a subterranean simmer
that swallows anger to fuel the flame
so it doesn't get its mouth washed out with soap
or thrown in a cold shower with clothes on
or hit with a wooden spoon.

Not fitting in, my four-year-old self ran away
set myself loose in the woods
let the willow tree be my mother
I swung in her arms and she taught me
how to flow and how to be flexible.

I played in the creek
organizing her stones in new melodies
and she taught me how to sing
washing away my loneliness
with her tadpoles and dragonflies.

At home, the summer hardens
I grow crooked, looking for those arms of love
with Jesus then drugs, then too much sugar
then sleeping with whomever, wherever, whenever.

Yesterday I went to the hot springs
that bubble up out of the ocean
offering her warm bath

when the tide is negative low.
The heat of the heart of the mother
welcomed my tears
as she marinated me
in pure love.

The cold of the ocean crashes around me
like the fear that sucks the heat away
I feel the depth of my fear, a primordial fear
of the dark, of the cold, of the alone.

This ongoing saga of fear versus love
as I titrate between cold ocean and hot spring,
I release myself from the warm arms of the mother
and plunge into the vast rhythm of the icy waves
following the wavy map of my thumbnail,
we are connected to everything.

Dark Whisperer

Welcome to the unknown, the deepest, darkest, unspoken, hidden, underground, underbelly, shadow self. You know, all the stuff we push away, the pain, the hurt, the shame, the fear, the longing, the desire, the dream. What we are rarely told is that the very stuff we push away and hide is where our power lives. When we bring that deep dark hidden stuff out into the light of day and pick through it, sifting and sorting, naming and claiming, we free up the energy we spent keeping it at bay. When we befriend the dark parts, forgive and reclaim the parts we could not love, we unearth the energy we need to fuel our creativity, our dreams, our life. A seed germinates in the dark earth because this darkness is where the juju lies. We think we are keeping ourselves safe by keeping secrets, but those secrets end up owning us and feeding on our life force. Whisper their names now, and they will whisper you back to life.

Body/Mindfulness: Grab your eye mask or scarf and place it over your eyes. Welcome the darkness. Close your eyes, settle in, and get comfy. Follow your breath as it flows in and out of your body. Arrive in yourself. Place a hand on your heart and a hand on your belly to help ground you. I'd like you to reach deep down into the place you usually don't go, you know, the dungeon, the cave, the no-trespassing zone, and notice if there's anything hiding in there that you feel like loving up. Do you have a secret you never tell? Have you swallowed or chained underground any experiences or memories, hoping they would go away? That's the territory we're entering. Please enter with kindness and respect. Only dig up what you feel ready to look at. OK, go ahead, take a look. What do you find there that's ready to be loved?

WRITE NOW! *Write about one or a few memories or experiences that have been hiding out in no-woman's land, your underground safe, locked away and forgotten. Is there a secret you feel ready to bring out and love? One, or a few, you feel ready to write about in a way that frees you up, deepens your understanding, reclaims your power, helps you integrate into wholeness? Be curious. Be gentle. Be respectful of yourself. There's a reason you've kept this secret hidden away. It has enormous power. Take your power back.*

Examples

TELL IT TO THE RIVER by Meredith Heller

> The barn on Travilah Road
> along the Potomac River in Maryland

where I made a home at thirteen
slept on the floor
with an old sleeping bag
from Salvation Army
hung a torn lace curtain
in the window
where the glass had long been broken.

I ate stale rye bread
from the trash
spent my quarters
on a tin of Medaglia d'Oro coffee
dark & sweet
like the beekeeper boy
I kissed behind the hive
for a jar of local honey
my skin buzzing,
Tell it to the river.

I was fifteen
living in a log cabin
in the foothills
of the Blue Ridge Mountains, Virginia
no electricity
no running water
with Willy, twenty-eight
who kicked around
in a pair of red Converse high-tops
pinned me to the hood of his station wagon
and held his hand over my mouth
so no one would hear me scream,
Tell it to the river.

I made bracelets
from copperhead snakes
I found dead on the road
taught myself to tan their skins
by slicing them open
scooping out their guts
once I found a baby bird inside
once a handful of fleshy eggs.

I'd nail the skins
to a wooden board
salt them and leave them
to dry in the sun
cut the skin into strips
sew them around a piece of rope
attached to a tube of beads I made
in a pattern called peyote stitch
I learned from the women
on the Navajo Reservation
I'd sell them in town for $20
which was a lot of food money
back then,
Tell it to the river.

The boy I met one summer
whose skin was made
of cinnamon sticks
who sat all day
at the water's edge
singing in a language
no one knew but me
we watched the water

braid the light in helixes
we made love
in a circle of pines
under a full moon
and three days later
we found his body;
suicide.
I crawled inside myself
and didn't speak
for many months
when I was a teen
on my own
trading my sex
for survival
my love
for belonging,
Tell it to the river.

My friend Annelies
eighty-eight-year-old Swiss artist
who simply is not old
she is tiny and strong
and determined as a beetle
hands constantly
making things
come to life
paper and glass
paint and clay.

She keeps bees
feeds the raccoons

cheats at cards
cusses worse than I do
when she loses
yodels expertly
and rides downhill
every morning on her kick-scooter
to swim in the pool.

She was my first true friend
she found me
when I was a lone wolf
my skin chewed raw
my fur full of sparks
slowly she shaped me
like one of her clay pots
into a human being
with a space inside
for homemade soup,
Tell it to the river.

To all the bards
along my path
who wonder where I go
when I go
who know me
as the wolf-hearted woman
with one eye dark
and one eye bright
one eye that looks inward
one that looks out
one that draws you closer
while the other

pushes you away,
Tell it to the river.

The way the water
loosens my hinges
turns my blood to opals
throws herself against me
purring like some wild beast
I rest my head against her chest
listen to her heartbeat:

> *yes, now*
>> *yes, now.*

The sun climbs the ridge
in the morning
and we howl together
because it's good to be alive
and say so,
Tell it to the river.

KEEPER OF SECRETS by Jo Walker

unformed clay
shattered glass
lone wolf's howl, tethered fast.

keeper of secrets
ink river stains
scribe of stories, for other names.

hummingbird hover
stormy stew
caterpillar death, no butterfly you.

WHAT ABOUT THE DARKNESS by Mireya Quirie

So for starters tell about the fear when Pop raged
violently, about Mom's black eye, about enforced silence,
about empty cupboards and food from the dumpster
behind Donut Alley, about sleeping on the park bench
and living at the motel and the campsites. And about
when he called you obese, disgusting.

But what about the nights backpacking, campfires under
the stars on the granite by the waterfall? What about the
singing, and the painting, and flying along the road on
the back of his bicycle?

Okay, well then, what about the forced blow job outside
your dorm? What about the beach party and saying
no, no; then leaving your body while he took what he
wanted, and how he called the next day to apologize?
Yeah, well, I told him *I was sorry*, so sorry, but he would
have to hear me now for all the assholes I never got to
say it to.

I told him how wrong he'd been to treat me that way.
That he would never see me again.
And he cried when I hung up the phone.

But also, there was my first love. And the many more
that followed. The ones who adored me, honored me,
offered me their open hearts, the ones who listened and
cared.

So what I want to say, where my deepest pain and
confusion come from now, is that when I hear the

news and read the history about military rapes, ethnic
cleansing, forced sterilization, I want to know where the
violence comes from. I want to know why there is such a
desperate need to desecrate women.

But then I know.
I know because I have felt my power.
When I speak with truth and experience and love. When
I dance and laugh with joy. When I make love. When I
carried and birthed my babies.

And I get it a little.
Such a fiercely beautiful power we hold.

How to Pray

What is prayer? What does prayer mean to you? Did you grow
up with organized religion, learning a specific way to pray?
Do you still pray in this way? Does it feel true for you? Does
it honor and feed your soul and connect you to something
bigger than yourself? Does it nourish you? Does it keep you
safe? What if we could make up our way to pray? How then
would you pray? I sang before I spoke, and I've always said
singing is how I pray. I still pray by singing. What if prayer
is aligning ourselves consciously with that deep presence in
the seat of our hearts, where we feel safe and held, at peace, at
home, connected to the great thrum of life. Let's reinvent, or
recommit to, how we pray. You in?

Body/Mindfulness: Get comfy. Close your beautiful eyes.
Say hello to the companionship of your breath. Place your
hands on your heart and give yourself some love. Take as

much time as you need until you feel yourself settle into stillness and arrive, feeling held in peace and belonging. With your hands resting on your heart, feel how you meet yourself with humble completeness. This is what prayer feels like to me. Sometimes *thank-you* is the greatest prayer we have. How do you pray?

WRITE NOW!   *Write what comes to mind when you consider prayer. What is prayer for you? Why and when and how do you pray? If you grew up with religion, learning a specific way to pray, do you still pray this way? Have you found other ways to pray? If you could make up your own way to pray, based on how you feel when you're deeply connected to yourself and source, how would you pray?*

Examples

ODE TO PRAYER by Victoria Moran

> Coming from Mexican, Irish & Italian families, I naturally began my journey with prayer at the young age of four years old in the basement of a Catholic church with my cousins making wooden crosses glued together from popsicle sticks, singing songs of Jesus.

> Mama & Papa left it up to Brother & me to choose our way of prayer while teaching us that God loves us & that we can speak to Him wherever because God is in Everything. You see, they did not want us to fear God as they had been taught.

> When I was a child & then a teenager, the forest preserves in Chicago became my church, lazily resting

on tall tree branches, caressing the texture of the brown
bark, watching closely the ants travel in their mighty
army to wherever home was for them.

Prayer came again inside the largest green plastic bowl
I'd ever seen, filled with maize & stories in Spanish,
surrounded by plump laughing women making tamales
for my best friend's quinceañera.

When I was seventeen prayer left me, or rather, I let
go of prayer in my teenage angst when I announced to
Mama that I was an atheist & she wept.

The following year my prayer life changed forever, once
I entered that dark womb in the Inipi of my Lakota
relatives and wonderment happenings occurred that
could not be explained by a rational, logical mind &
a girl had a meltdown while I sat at the feet of the
medicine man asking a million questions to his chagrin
& delight.

Prayer came again in the form of movement that my
Senegal relatives taught me, using my hips & my booty
& my legs, they taught me how to fly through the air, to
land gently on my tippy-toes so as to kiss the earth with
my holy feet.

Prayer came again while cleaning my brother's body.
Anointing him with oils of myrrh & frankincense while
singing incantations & listening to bagpipes & bellows
like our ancestors once did in Cork, Ireland.

Prayer came again in the Amazon with her river spells & pink dolphins, a viny brew that held mysteries of the universe that only the Great Mother could breathe & whisper.

Prayer came again in the lesser-known spaces in Puna, where my woman clan gathered in naturally occurring lava-formed saunas, singing women's songs in call & response, laughing & cooing at the marvel of who we were.

Prayer came again during Devi Bhava amid a thousand bodies swaying to Bhajans, drinking hot chai & waiting for Mama Amma to embrace & hold our hearts & our hurts in hers all the while murmuring into my ear: "My daughter, my daughter, my daughter."

Prayer came again in the hidden recesses of Golden Gate Park that lovingly consoled my broken heart while I walked pain-ridden & frightened.

Prayer came again as I worked with La Mesa & listened to my Quero relatives share the teachings of the ancient despacho & what true reciprocity feels like in my golden sun heart.

Prayer came again during Shabbat with my Jewish relatives passing the overflowing cup of red wine, singing blessings with our hands over eyes touching the warm challah, reminding us that we are all connected through nourishment.

And now, at my altar, Lady of Guadalupe alight, rosary
in hand, made of antique beads of red & white roses,
I murmur the prayer in rhythm to His Sacred Heart,
united with the faith of my youth & my lineages finally
landing, swathed in sacred communion with Him. A
reunion, a coming home. A blessed full arc.

HOW I PRAY by Karen Burt-Imira

I got lucky, no one ever taught me to pray.
My dear body found prayer on her own
my own language spilled out over my tongue
sliding and gliding beyond my lips
from the fertile hollows of my throat.
My heart reaching and teaching
loud callings to canyon walls
redwood towers and ocean foam
softer incantations to silver-lined roses
and sweet sleepy children.

Yes, my heart taught me
to prepare a plentiful table
for the honored guest of
All My Relations
a welcoming table of tones
sculpted sounds
bellows and beauty
notes arising from
my expectant womb of
spontaneous creation.

Every prayer a new labor of love
a new birth hinting at possibilities

and longings
and love
with fresh, wide-open
innocence.

Too Much Is Just Enough

Ever been told you're too much? Too intense, too deep, too wild, too weird, too fierce, too sexual, too aggressive, too brainy, too difficult, too big, too bossy? Yeah, me too. And in response, we learned to make ourselves small so we'd fit in. Survive. Belong. So no one would hurt our feelings and squash our morale by telling us we're wrong and bad for spilling out of the container. I'm here to tell you there was never anything wrong or bad with your too-muchness; it was the container that was too dang small. So let's reclaim our too-muchness, shall we? *Muchness* is just enough. Muchness is about plenty and abundance and yes and overflowing with something to share. If you've got muchness, too-muchness, you've got the goods.

Body/Mindfulness: Cozy in and close your eyes. Allow your breath to find you. Ride the waves, in and out. How does it feel in there? Without needing to change or fix anything, just notice your experience. Is it spacious? Do you feel free to be yourself? Do you meet yourself and like who you are? Take a good deep breath and fill yourself up with the sense of who you are, all of you. Are you a lot? I hope so. Reflect on the ways you were told you were too much, and in response, made yourself small in order to be accepted and loved. Then ask what it would feel like to give yourself permission to be the muchness you truly are.

WRITE NOW! *Write about the ways you were made to feel you were too much. Write about how you made yourself small so you'd belong. Write about what it feels like to break free of that smallness and inhabit the muchness that you are. What does it feel like to allow yourself to be too much? To take up too much space, to speak your mind too much, to be too brilliant, too sexy, too strong, too fierce, too intense, too deep, too direct, too big, too bossy? Feels pretty good, right? Write about who you are when your muchness is the right amount of enoughness.*

Examples

POLLYANNA BE DAMNED! by Mary Pritchard

I am who I am —
don't judge me for my too-muchness!
Don't mock my too-muchness!
Too kind, too giving, too caring,
too many smiles, too damn sweet!

Passion, courage, vulnerability
pour down and through me
as I reach out to others with my too-muchness,
Pollyanna be damned!

I find the gold, the glimmering moonlight
hiding within others
I am the bestower of joy
I pierce the heart of the sorrowful soul
I mend the pain of the broken child.

Let my giver receive
let my helper find solace

untether my too-muchness
nourish my naked, hungry heart.

Let me unearth my beautiful too-muchness
and set to work giving hope
to my sorrowful soul
embracing my inner child
letting the golden goodness
feed and nourish my too-muchness,
Pollyanna be damned!

TOO MUCH! by Jeannie McKenzie

You are too much!
Over the top!

Some days
I do too much
of nothing

Just sit and listen
to water pouring over rocks
feel the sun beat down on my body

Too curious
to accept anything
at face value

I want to understand why
and how to listen more deeply
until I know

How the heart of the universe
is an ever-evolving creation
through you and me and all life

Maybe that's going too far
or not far enough
I will defend my too-outspoken

too-rebellious
too-weird perspective
by exploring further

the depths of what is
just too silly
I am too assertive

not to follow my own path
and too sensitive
not to choose love.

CHAPTER 7

Belonging

*Weave the abandoned parts of yourself
back into belonging.*

Belonging is as necessary to our survival as food, shelter, and safety. We are tribal beings. We need and want each other. We long to be included in the clan, to live in interdependence, and to participate in the natural tides of giving and receiving. Even those of us who prefer being alone seek belonging, whether to self, place, or something bigger than us. Ironically, I recently heard of an online group of women loners. Perhaps even loners crave a sense of belonging with other loners. So what is belonging? What does it mean, and what does it feel like to belong? For some of us, the sense of belonging is so natural we don't even question it, but for others, the orphans, outcasts, rebels, and loners, the separateness and loneliness of not belonging, not fitting in, not finding one's tribe, can cut holes in the fabric of self. Let's look at four main areas of belonging: to self, to others, to community, and to something larger than ourselves. We need all four of these to help us roll smoothly through life. Consider each area of belonging, and notice which ones feel engaged and which ones could use some tending.

Four Main Areas of Belonging

- Belonging to self
- Belonging to others: family, partner, children, parent, sibling, friend, pet
- Belonging to community or place
- Belonging to something bigger than us: God, spirit, life force, nature

Where I'm From

Where does our sense of belonging come from? How do we learn what belonging is or what it feels like? How do we discern healthy from unhealthy belonging? Let's go back to our childhoods to unearth the people, places, activities, experiences, and things that helped shape our first sense of belonging, good or bad. From here we can make informed choices about to what and to whom we belong. Shall we?

Body/Mindfulness: Close your eyes and cozy in. Follow the tides of your breath. Allow yourself to soften, open, and arrive in your inner world. Place a hand on your belly and a hand on your heart to help support you as you travel back to your childhood. Imagine yourself as a child. Call up an image of yourself, or simply sense into yourself as a child. Allow one or a few memories to surface, good or bad, that gave you a feeling of belonging. Trust what arises. Gather the details. Notice people, places, activities, and things that elicited a sense of belonging in you.

WRITE NOW! *Write about the people, places, activities, and things you belonged to as a child. How did this sense of belonging* *shape and influence how you meet your need for connection and belonging?*

Examples

REACH & RIDE by Kelli Mulligan

> I come from small-town farmers,
> beekeepers, a quaint furniture store,
> within a vast, dry land,
> where God is a man, and we obey.
>
> I come from Elaine and Tim,
> eager to leave, learn, live
> in a different kind of small town,
> trading scalped earth for redwood trees,
> education for land rights.
>
> I come from parents who settled in Napa,
> the upside-down world
> between pesticide city
> and country living.
>
> I come from people
> who married young,
> broke each other's hearts
> and still love one another.
>
> A mom who married my dad's friend
> and a dad who married a person
> who remains only half available.
>
> I come from pulling up
> all the straps of all the boots,

burying fear in laundry,
being good but knowing
I was meant to get the fuck out.

I come from a long line
of stubborn, scorned women
and I am breaking the cycle.

I am not your snow bunny.
I wear sensible shoes
and I've come to throw down
in this arena.

I come from almond trees,
ATVs with three wheels, four wheels,
on-the-side wheels,
and my six-year-old self
put it upright because
if you can reach, you can ride.

I come from suppressing myself,
minimizing myself to make others comfortable
like flimsy slippers in a rich hotel,
love them or leave them
but please don't bring them home.

I come from the depths of the earth
and erupt like a motherfucking volcano
that could not keep her crust together.
So I blew long and hard
until I was whole again.

I come from my people,
my souls and my kin,
here before me, here after me.
Here together, in this moment
with self, with everyone,
with everything. I come!

WHERE I'M FROM by Mireya Quirie

I am from bold and daring, stepping timidly over
railroad ties across the San Lorenzo. Waves crashing in
my pounding heart, eyes upturned to my father's bright,
encouraging face, his hand holding mine so tightly I
knew I was safe. And emboldened, I dared! I crossed
the tracks to the beach below. I am from those same
eyes, glaring, when I dared to contradict him, shaming,
derisive, warning, terrifying eyes.

I am from dark nights, gathered around the bed, scissors
and string boiling in the pot to tie around an umbilical
cord. Home births, the grip of my mother's hand tight
on mine as she moaned and pushed.

I am from siblinghood, rich and fragrant as compost.
Bedrooms tight and full. Two sisters and four brothers
whom I watched be born into this world, mine. My
first babies. The smell of them. The smell of my mother.
Sitting next to her as she nursed them. Their diapers,
their baths. The airplanes, zoom zoom! Open your
mouth, eat up! My most special people. Holding them,
treasuring them, bossing them around, comforting them.
Telling them I loved them. They'll never know how
much.

I am from novenas, from rosary beads held in my
hands around the fireplace, please God in heaven, find
a home for us. Staying in friends' homes. Staying in
motels. Sleeping on benches, sleeping in cars, sleeping
in campsites. I am from sandwiches from the nuns,
government cheese, donuts from the dumpster. Boxes
of food from St. Vincent de Paul. From garbage bags of
cast-off neighbors' clothes. From shame, from retreat, to
an inside safe place.

I am from helping in the kitchen. Making biscuits.
Making cake. Setting the table, washing the dishes,
ironing the napkins. The flowers my mother grew and
cut and put in tiny vases around the house. The comfort
in the songs she sang to me in bed. The ache of my
father's voice in the songs he sang and played on guitar
and piano. The games, the laughing, the yelling. The
bruises, the blisters, the blackberries we picked and put
into huge cobblers we politely and respectfully scarfed,
after the prayers had been said.

I am from starry skies, sandals, and exhausting,
exhilarating trails. Sierra campfires and warm cans of
chili. Beyond electricity, stove, refrigerator. Bears tearing
our bags from the trees, eating every piece but one
of my cinnamon gum. The hot meal we devoured on
completing the trail. Happiness. I am from being out
there, out there with God, the only truth I know.

Permission

Permission?! We're adults, we don't need no stinkin' permission. And yet we do. We really, truly do. We need permission

to be ourselves, to make mistakes and learn, to be a mess and fall apart, to rest and replenish when we're used up. We need permission to stop apologizing for our brilliance, bravery, strength, love. We need permission to change. We need permission for our self-expression, our creativity, our cycles of fallow and fruitful. We need permission for our belonging, connection, fulfillment, and joy. We need permission to dream big. We need permission to be exactly who we are.

There was a Facebook video that went viral about a little girl, three years old, who goes into the bathroom and comes out with lipstick on, or as she calls it, "yipick." Her dad grills her lovingly about where she got the lipstick: Is it hers or her mother's? He probes, "Did you ask anyone if you could put that lipstick on?" And she answers candidly, "I asked myself!" This always cracks me up but also hits home in a big way. I ask you now, what do you need to ask yourself and give yourself permission for?

Body/Mindfulness: Close your eyes and settle in. Allow your breath to breathe you as your body softens and opens. Place your hand on your belly or anywhere else on your body that feels supportive and nourishing. Tune in and ask yourself if there's something, anything, you could use your own permission for. Is there some way you hold out on yourself, hold yourself down, hold yourself back from expressing who you are and what you truly want? Welcome what arises with curiosity and kindness, and then ask and give yourself permission for whatever it is you want.

WRITE NOW! *Write about what you're giving yourself permission for. Dig deep and pull at the roots of how you've held yourself back and how now you can ask and give yourself permission,* *like the little girl in the video: "I asked myself!" Go ahead, give yourself permission to be true to yourself and see how it weaves you deeper into belonging. Write from either first or second person — I give you permission or You have my permission — whichever gets it flowing for you.*

Examples

PERMISSION by Karen Burt-Imira

> I give myself
> and anyone who wants to join me
> *PERMISSION*
> to rant & rage
> to break some teeth & necks
> with words that slice & bite
> chew & spit
> kick hard.
>
> Who gave permission to burn the Amazon?
> Who gave permission to poison living soil, fresh wind,
>   pure water?
> Who gave permission to spread lies brazenly for profit &
>   power?
> Who gave permission for greed?
> Who gave permission to traffic babies and film them
>   being raped & beaten?
> Who gave permission to enjoy that and say "the bloodier,
>   the better!"?
> Who gave permission to the KKK to lynch? And bring
>   children to watch?
> Who gave permission for slavery that continues on and
>   on and on?
> Who gave permission for cruelty to run free?

What has all this got to do with giving permission
to my ragged voice to sing beautiful songs?

Permission for cruelty is a thorn stuck deep in my throat
a tightening noose around my diaphragm,
a howl and a shriek
a thousand-year-long scream —
NOOOOOOO!

Oh yes, my body is trauma informed,
at times contorted & deformed from despair.

So I give my ragged voice permission to sing
beautiful songs, to make joyful sounds
to speak in tongues from my own territories.

Because this duality is my humanity
I give myself permission to crack open
from fear and grief and fury
I give myself permission to break open wide
with joy and purpose and love.

PERMISSION by Ellis McNichol

Permission. The word a prayer I reach for tangled in the
wind. To be a wild, holy, uncontained mess. In wide-open
spaces and the vastness of flesh. Knife at my hip, gray ash
on my fig cheeks. Dozens of nights I made myself too
caged and small and clipped to demand more from being.

Salt-sprinkled screams that tremble in G-minor, G-spot
trauma down the interstate as I fly, flutter and crash,

alone, into the womb of a cave. Dripping and panting
with the juices of exit wounds in damp dank dark,
where birds don't fly, a double-headed snake greets a
crushed mind and broken bones I left years ago, and
slithers to settle in what was a spine. I hold my breath
and wait to die.

But suddenly the snake is dancing in the dust of my
complacency, now rising up like a cello cry wolf howl,
inspired by the movement of new songs. She slithers up
me like a vine, emerges by mouth and murmurs: "Never
again place your destiny in someone else's hands." The
rope a split tongue on fire, ember shooting star rippling
up and down a charred sparked log. I return to the
flames of holy mess. The Rosaceae family. Sparrows. To
remember remembrance.

Gardening again, I finger soil horizons and gather
thoughts for poetry from trees. Where does this mystery
come from? I wonder, as hawthorn bushes explode
between bare toes and forest service roads to slice open
my knee. I forgive them, and myself. For floundering,
forgetting every single lesson, breaking promises and
flesh. Ripping out feathers, self-abuse rotting in a decade
of denial and brine. I'm bent and swaying at the roses of
my hips ravished by men. I whisper in waterfall: freedom
is rarely only beautiful. The snake hisses with two
mouths, and I hiss back.

At night I rub calendula poultices across bloody stumps
where wings used to be. The bird in me demands rebirth,

as insistent to live as weeds. I rage in liquid metal alchemy.
A storm cloud spreads across the war zone of my back,
where parched scars sip and delight in any water. The
furnace of courage aches for open skies and shattering grief
healing. I scream, riding 95 down the Milky Way interstate
until my throat is stripped raw, begging for an end. I
scream until sound is nearly lost. A petal whisper, fading
and childlike. And then, when the dust drapes my bones,
I scream again. Until blood pools in crescent moons at the
corner of my lip. And I unfurl budding wings drenched in
war paint. Brave, suddenly.

Permission. The word a nest I build from reclaimed limbs
in flowering trees. To endure each mountain crumble.
That I may always remember my backbone. Permission,
despite decay and disaster, to swallow wildflower honey
and sing. As though all I've ever known is this kindness
and flight.

I Have Come Here To ...

Is there anything you've been neglecting that feeds your soul
like nothing else? A lot of our sense of belonging comes from
doing what we love, what feeds our soul, what we came here
to do. And if we're not doing it, not doing what brings us joy
and purpose, we feel lost, disconnected, depressed, and this
diminishes our sense of belonging. Let's discover and reclaim
what we've come here to do. When we start doing what we
truly love, we usually find our tribe, and everything in our
life starts to flow and the magic of the universe finds us. Let's
write ourselves back into belonging to self, community, and
something bigger than us.

What have you come here to do? Here are some ideas from my workshop participants to spark your remembering. I have come here to: dance, sing, play an instrument, ride my bike, learn to fly a plane, rock climb, swim with dolphins, hike the Himalayas, say no, say yes, build a house, travel the world, work with the dying, work with the ones being born, grow a successful business, serve a cause I believe in, help children or animals or the earth, heal myself, heal others, be selfish, be beautiful, be a mess, make love however I want with whomever I want, not care one hoot what anyone thinks of me, wear a party dress at 10 a.m. to the grocery store, spend the day in my pajamas, spend the day in the nude, buy myself a present, make a present for someone I like, give away all my possessions, move to a city, move to the country, live on sailboat, spend a week in silence or darkness, learn to speak another language, write a song, write a book, take a painting or pottery class, make a contribution to science or medicine. What inspires and feeds your soul? What have you come here to do?

Body/Mindfulness: Close your eyes and cozy in. Allow your body to soften and open as you follow your breath, in and out. Place a hand on your heart and listen as though your hand were a great ear that hears the deepest longings of your soul. What do you hear? What do you know? What did you come here to do?

WRITE NOW! *Write about what you heard from your heart about what you came here to do. Write about one thing, or write about many. What brings you joy and purpose? What helps you belong to self, others, life?*

Examples

NAKED VOICE by Lauren Montgomery

> I am calling back my naked, authentic voice.
>
> I have come here to sing.
> I need all of me to sing.
> Not just the voice who
> knows which key,
> to hit the perfect fifth,
> not the small voice
> who remembers
> which note comes next,
> but the deep, rich voice
> the one who echoes
> from the sacred caverns
> of my soul.
>
> I have come here to sing
> the voice who booms
> with ancient thunder,
> rich and wet with rain.
>
> The voice who curls and rushes
> and pools and collects herself
> deep down
> beneath the ground.
>
> The voice who is always here,
> even when the earth above
> is parched and cracked,
> and ravaged by fire.

There is a pure, sweet,
resonant sound
that gurgles up
from places
no one can see.

She is pure,
but not always pretty,
she takes her sweet time.

She listens first,
and receives,
the hollow, empty moan
of her aching heart.

She then rushes out
from rocky mountainsides,
pours down like rain,
she is there,
even when no one else believes.

She will hold you like a newborn,
feed you from her own body.

She will birth the sweet naked truth
of my soul.

STARFISH by Laurie McMillan

I have come here to stretch long and wide like a cat into
a field of sunflowers to be a sanctuary, a communion
calling back the wonder girl by the ocean who once
stepped rock to rock unworried — a starfish, trusting

the heart, not the wrinkled brow, only arms, wide arms,
the stretch calls to the unconscious signaling ultimate
freedom remembered connection with mother, father,
friend, dream, world, wish —

So much to call back, but the stretch is the invitation,
and it is all I need to ask my worlds, my dreams to
return. I call back hope. The fragility of it as it swings
back and forth, dizzy on a wire. I make a place for it next
to my heart. Hope, heart, hope, heart.

I have come here to make the roundtable for others so
they can speak freely. To wail, to confess, to dream, to
talk to themselves. I stretch out to include what fear
wants to tell me, which is to let go of it. Keep stretching.
You won't break.

Move in rings as if you were circling like a hawk. Wide
wings. Orange tipped. Looking across to the horizon
that stretches too. We make ourselves into boxes, not
starfish. Too small. Captured. Collected. The stretch frees
us, moves us into the unknown to explore the layers of
stretching into infinity.

Why I Write

There have been times in my life when the only place I could
find belonging was in my writing. Writing has saved my life
and woven me back into belonging more times than I can tell
you. I write because I believe spirit listens for the places where
we love and own ourselves, and one of the best ways I know
to get there is through writing. In my workshops, we find belonging to ourselves through writing and sharing our poems.

We find belonging to whatever it is that muses us, igniting and humming our blood like a beehive, making wild honey with our words. We find belonging to community as we share our pieces, cross-pollinating, mirroring, being witnessed, received, acknowledged. We find belonging when sharing ourselves bravely and vulnerably, knowing we are welcomed exactly as we are. You've been writing for a while now, yes? On your own, along with this book, or in community, and so I ask you, why do you write? What happens for you when you write? Do you unearth the treasure, turn pain into pearls, feel plugged in and connected to something greater than you when you write?

Body/Mindfulness: Close your beautiful eyes and settle in. Ride the waves of your breath as you arrive inside yourself. Place your hand on your heart, and ask yourself, Why do I write? What happens for me when I write? How do I feel when I write? What do I connect with in myself when I write? What am I tapping into? What do I learn by writing? Why the heck do I write?! And then listen to what bubbles up in you in response.

WRITE NOW! *Write all the ideas, feelings, sensations, and emotions that arise for you when you ask yourself why you write. Pour it all onto the page, every last drop! You can shape it later if you wish. Notice what happens for you while you write; include the awareness of your process as you write. Be ready to discover something you didn't know you knew. How does writing weave you back into belonging to yourself and life? Write as literally, metaphorically, logically, or magically as you wish. You might say, for example, writing gives me gills so I can breathe underwater. Or writing helps me name, sort, and express my feelings so I come out clean and new. Put your pen to paper, and don't stop writing until you've unearthed every treasure of understanding, insight, and discovery of why you write. Go!*

Examples

WHY I WRITE by Lauren Montgomery

I write to take off the wrapper.
Because I want to taste the sweetness inside.
I want to lick the sugar that has crystallized
somewhere I can't see.
I write because I'm tongue-tied.
I write to watch the waves of thoughts crash into each other
and draw themselves back into the sea.
I write to find myself.
I write because I am lost.
I write to come home.
I write to paint pictures of secret places
and to see things with fresh eyes.
I write for oxygen, to breathe life,
to make space for the parts of me that ache.
I write to heal.
I write to form rhyme and rhythm
meaning and melody
from a world of madness.
I write to make sense
of things that feel broken,
and to sew them whole again.

WHY I WRITE by Kelli Mulligan

I write my map on sand and paper.
The sandy parts blow away in light wind
the ones on paper stay forever.

I write to breathe, deep as a bellow
inhaling to ignite the wildfires that burn in me.

Exhaling to create new space for fertile grounds
where grasses and trees grow from my ashen soil.

I write to peer underneath the layers
of my skin and blood, past the bones
to the electric energy that pumps me alive
where my dark meets my light
in crevices rarely seen and felt.

I write to take off the cloak
that was given to me as a child.
She wore it until it wore her down
to the ground where the dry bones
can be found.

I write because beauty is so BIG
and I must follow its path
back to the center
where my soul and my pen
flip between dreams
meeting on paper.

I write to soar up above the valleys,
catching thermal winds high and low
letting them take me where I am meant to go.
I do not always know where,
but I will write, I will take flight.

Chant for Belonging

We can call ourselves home, you know. We can reach out with
our hearts and voices to the four elements, our ancestors, our
animal allies, our muse; to nature, life force, the universe. We

can send out a chant, a rhythmic singsong phrase of poetic words, like a magic spell, and marry ourselves back into belonging. Ready?

Body/Mindfulness: Settle in and close your eyes. Feel the surface underneath and behind you supporting you as your body begins to soften and melt open. Allow your breath to find you, and ride the waves in and out. Arrive in yourself. Place a hand on your heart and a hand on your belly or anywhere else that feels supportive and nurturing. Listen now inside until you hear a chant or a song bubbling up in you. These heart/soul songs are usually pure and simple. Nothing too fancy or complicated. They rise directly from source in a universal language. Can you hear it now, a chant or song calling you home?

WRITE NOW! *Write the chant or song that calls you home. Write a chant for what you belong to. Write as much or as little as you like. It may be a long winding ballad or a short potent spell with a repeating chorus line. Anything goes. Your song, your chant, your call home.*

Examples

ASANA OF BELONGING by Korynn Amm

> Exhale...
> Releasing the flesh from my bones
> unfolding tiny crevices of curiosity
> holding my dreams between.
>
> Exhale...
> Swimming through my veins
> making music with myself

permission to play
to stay here
breathing
being
sinking
deep into the feathers
lifting ... drifting ...

Exhale ...
Painting streaks with my sweat
dripping down into my roots
grasping at my heart
just to finally feel

beating ...
    beating ...
        beating ...
Exhale ...
Holding myself here
making love to myself
and now I know
what this feels like —
belonging,
forcing nothing.

I BELONG by Kelli Mulligan

I belong to my people,
old and young
our eyes have met before.

I belong to the earth,
alive below my toes
and above my head.

I belong to my body,
fingertips, retinas,
voice.

I belong to my bravery,
jumping off
and out.

I belong to purpose,
creating safe space
to learn and be.

I belong to my ghosts,
I lay them to rest.
I ask them for help.

I belong to my fears,
and I eat them, one piece at a time
until they make me strong.

I belong to my peace,
my breath, my faith, my hope
my ability to help myself and others along the way.

I belong to my writing,
mapping my stories
of love and loss.

I belong to myself,
deep-blue waters
running within and pouring out of me.

CHAPTER 8

Fertile Darkness

Journey into the heart of the inward cycle.

Many of us grow up learning to fear the dark. We don't know exactly what lurks there, so we fear it. We fear both the literal dark, like nighttime, nocturnal animals, and nightmares, and the metaphorical dark, like depression, anger, our shadow self, the deep psyche, the unknown, and the fallow part of our cycle. This fallow part doesn't get talked about much. It's what I call the great undoing. It involves shedding the belief that our worth is based solely on our accomplishments, our doings. We get tricked into being human doings rather than human beings. There is a cultural taboo against not doing, against simply being. Just being is challenging for most of us. We try to fill the emptiness, numb it, hide from it, escape it. People often ask, "Are you keeping busy?" And I think, why would I want to be busy? It takes bravery and discipline to let go, unwind, unhinge, disassemble, dissolve into the great darkness, the unknown, the nothingness, the mystery. This is the fertile darkness of being from which everything new is birthed. So what lives in the dark? Seeds, worms, mycelia, embryos, stars. As we reclaim our relationship with the dark, we discover that darkness is the source from which all new life, creativity, insight, ideas, invention, and dreams arise. All seeds, literal and metaphorical, birth and incubate in the fertile darkness. Let's go now to the hidden space that lives beneath the surface.

Brave Undoing

All things in nature, and that includes us, have a resting time, a fallow, empty, dark, undoing un-time, when they cease doing and simply *be*. Let's enter the dark phase, shall we? Let's fold into the great undoing before spring wakes us, calling us back to the world of light and doings. Let's drop our roots deep into the darkness and sup on the nourishment of un-doingness, so that when the doingness returns, and it will, it always does, we rise rested and rejuvenated. When we make room for the dark part of our cycle, we learn to trust the whole process. We know we will rise again, because it's the natural way of things, but before the new project is birthed, there is simply being. In the simplicity of being we are renewed. Let's soften and melt into beingness and discover the treasure that resides there. It takes bravery and often rebellion and discipline to hang with the darkness. Shall we?

Body/Mindfulness: Grab your eye mask or scarf and place it over your eyes so you can immerse yourself in the dark. Close your eyes and get comfy. Arrive in the darkness of your inner being. Allow your breath to find you and breathe you. Ride the waves as you soften and melt into the vast terrain of your dark inner cosmos. Say hello. Notice what it feels like to simply be here and breathe without doing anything else. Is this easy or challenging for you? Just notice, without judgment. Keep coming back to being. Each time you find yourself wanting to do something, say, yes, I understand, and then return to simply being. It takes practice to undo the programming of doing. Stay with it. Each time you bring yourself back to being, you strengthen your capacity to simply be, like strengthening a muscle. You learn to give in to beingness. Breathe into beingness. Be with being.

WRITE NOW! *Write about your process of allowing yourself simply to be. It takes a special kind of bravery and focus to not do anything. Do you struggle to let go and do nothing? Do you have to fight your impulses to get up and do something? Does simply being challenge everything you've ever learned about basing your self-love on your accomplishments and achievements? Be patient with yourself. We are undoing a lifetime of conditioning. Or perhaps being comes naturally to you. You're able to melt and slip easily into undoing, like ice in the sun. Write about your experience with beingness.*

Examples

HOW BRAVE I AM by Geneva Toland

How brave I am to ask for help
and then receive, receive, receive
until I have overstayed my welcome
and then, receive some more.

How brave I am for undoing
patterns of perfection,
of overachievement
of go, go, go,
of never enough,

and then flailing
and flopping like a fish
plopped on the deck,
just learning for the
first time how to

b r e a t h e

How brave I am to say: I want this.
I want to be seen.
I want to live my gifts,
and then to say, well,
I'm doing the best I can

and sitting my ass down
to watch a truly terrible television show
because the day is done
and I am tired, and lord,
I am good enough.

BRAVE UNDOING by Laurie McMillan

How brave I am to come to the writing desk every
morning as if it were a party, that's right, there's music
and backup singers and a crazy drummer all playing in
the heart, and deep in those chambers are bells signifying
truth: "Wake up, be here now."

Undoing the pain of coming to the page like it was work,
a job, instead knowing it is nothing, no thing, but the
party of essence and discovery, of letting go and undoing
what I think I know to get to the truth in the dark soil
where the sprouts are coming up, where the seeds are just
starting to turn green.

Part of me, the part that has standards and expects so
much, is undoing to meet the night and the fertile
longing. Letting the body soften opens life, the limitless
space inside. Every morning at the writing desk, I boogie

and holler as the pen flows and the words sizzle and scat across the page. Party!

How brave I am to stop self-torture, page counts, lines written, chapters done. Undo and become one with creation right here and now in the space that is nothing. Unlearning, undoing, I forget who I am again and again, so I can write myself into existence.

Come, Vulture

Meet vulture, the great ally of death and resurrection. The circling, cycling black scavenger bird who sniffs out death, feasts on decay, picks the bones clean. That might sound disgusting, but these birds are doing holy work. They are the great recyclers, cleaning and alchemizing death into life. They are dark angels. We should be grateful for the vultures who do this dirty work. Let's invite vulture to come feast on anything and everything we're ready to let go. Let's trust the dark cycle and the great guardian vultures who help it along. Vulture helps us let go, recycle, rebirth. What are you ready to let go of? What in you is dying and needs to be released and recycled into something new?

Body/Mindfulness: Settle in and close your eyes. Give yourself to the dark. Breathe along with the tides of your breath as they fill and empty you. Even breathing is a form of living and dying. A doing and a letting go. Place a hand on your belly and a hand on your heart and ask yourself: What's dying in me that I am ready to let go? Perhaps you're ready to let go of doubt, fear, anger, apathy, addiction, depression, exhaustion, negative self-talk, unfulfilling relationships, loneliness, isolation, unrewarding work. Imagine offering these things to the great vultures to be devoured and picked clean, freeing up the energy, making it available for something new.

WRITE NOW! *Write a list of the things you're ready to let go. Then write a poem calling vulture to come devour what's rotting and to recycle it into something new, something better, something more beautifully alive.*

Examples

COME FEAST ON ME by Lauren Montgomery

> Come feast on me, great sky beast —
> where I am numb, dead
> where the flesh of my dreams
> clings, rotting on my bones.
>
> Let me feed your hunger —
> come, eat my weakness
> this dragging, empty hole
> that has collapsed me
> from within.
>
> Feed yourself on me —
> chew carefully,
> the aching legs of my desires,
> my longing to "become."
>
> Eat my head, my eyes,
> my brain, my tears.
> I have been so confused
> with seeing, choosing,
> believing I was dying.

Eat the darkness that covers my eyes,
eat the sickness that clamps my heart.

I will wake from this dream.
I will be sick no more!

DARK ANGELS by Geneva Toland

I feed my wasted love to the vultures

Dark angels,
dip your skulls to my breast

Tear my blouse open and pick
my ribs clean
Turn my naked face to the sky
where stars slip through my eye sockets

If I can't give myself to you
If I can't be devoured by
your hands on my hips
your mouth on my thighs

Then surely someone
should feed on this wasted love

Feed it to the vultures, where life will grow
from their bellies of rottenness

Where death is nothing but
a breakfast feast

Their slick tongues sucking marrow from my bones,
I cry out — empty me!

In spring perhaps there will be more to me, yet
without you, who knows —

For now I cannot imagine being anything
but space and bone.

Blackout Poems

Blackout poems are a hands-on way to engage with the great
mystery and create something from nothing. They are an exciting, tangible way to see what emerges from the dark unknown.
You'll need a few pages of text from an old book, magazine,
newspaper, or manual, or you can print a page of anything,
maybe a poem, yours or someone else's. Bring a thick dark
marker or crayon and a pencil. Here we go!

How to Make a Blackout Poem: Take your page of text, and
without reading through it, allow words to jump off the page
and catch your attention. Any words. Words you like. Words
that inspire you, make you happy, make you laugh. Evocative
words, sad words, words you find juicy just because. Circle
about ten to twenty of these words with your pencil. Don't
think about the order of the words, or a storyline, or needing
to be logical. Just circle the words you like and see what presents itself. Be willing to allow the emerging poem or story to
be sparse, without connective tissue, without needing to make
sense. Trust the mystery. The poem knows the poem. Read
through the words you circled in the order they appear on
your page. Does a storyline emerge organically from the words
you circled? With blackout poems, we tell the story with what
lies between the words, through the dark space, what's not
said, what lives and breathes in the underground of the piece.
Now take your marker or crayon and color in everything except the words you circled. Abracadabra!

Examples

EUPHORIA by Lisa Eddy

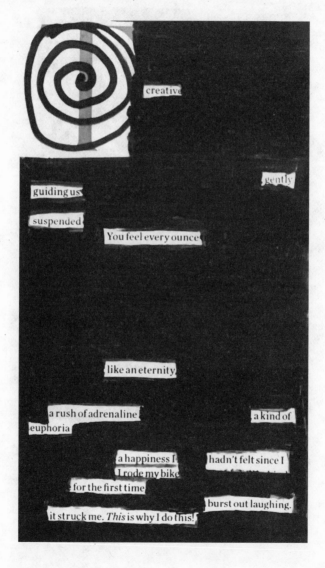

RIPE FRUIT by Korynn Amm

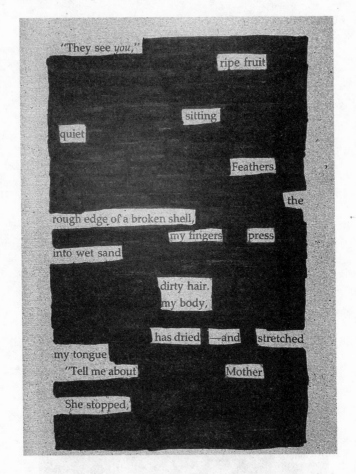

WILDERNESS by Mireya Quirie

WILDERNESS

the sun had softened
safe and rapid progress

an ice cascade
shattered
by deep, blue
To thread my way

I endeavored

compelling

warm enough

thus enabling me

Continuing

this glacier is easy
armed with an axe

beautifully

WILD MUSIC by Mary Pritchard

Dark Totem

In the dark it helps to have a guide, a companion, a totem. Though most of us journey the dark alone, and in many ways we need to, to develop the grit to survive, there is nothing like having a friend in the darkness. And what friend can you really count on to be there with you in the dark? Most people are too busy with the light to surrender to the dark, but not animals and magical beings, for they know the dark holds treasure. Animals know from rest and sleep and having days when nothing gets done. They trust that the dark mystery of undoing is as necessary to health and productivity as being on top of our game. So let's call up a dark totem, an animal or magical companion to help us inhabit, journey, and harvest the treasure of the dark.

Body/Mindfulness: Get cozy. Close your beautiful eyes. Settle in and feel supported by what's underneath and behind you, allowing your body to soften and open as you make yourself at home in the rich darkness of your being. Find your breath, and ride the waves in and out as you sink deeper into your inner world. Place a hand on your heart and a hand on your belly to help ground and center you. Journey with me now to meet your dark totem. Clear your mind and ask your heart or spirit to send you a wise and benevolent ally who knows how to navigate the dark. It may be an animal, a person, or any kind of creature, real or magical. Whoever or whatever shows up, be curious. Say hello. Notice how you feel with them. Trust what you feel. If for any reason you don't like who shows up, send them back and ask for another guide. When you feel solid about your totem, ask for their guidance and support as you journey through the dark. Some things you might ask for help with are health, relationships, self-acceptance, healing, purpose, understanding, forgiveness. You might ask for assistance with depression, anger, loneliness, grief, sorrow, loss, addiction. Listen with your whole being, and absorb the message of your totem. They may communicate in words, images, or feelings. You may simply share a kind of knowing. Trust the help and wisdom you receive. Thank them. Ask if you can call on them again.

WRITE NOW! *Write about your experience with your dark totem. Who are they, what do they look like, how do you feel in their presence, how do they communicate with you, what wisdom do they share? Write all the details you can remember from your journey.*

Examples

FREA'S CLAN by Nicole Phillips

> We must be nimble nomads, timber wolf says.
> We shall survive, light-footed wild hunters.
> Frea's spirit comes to me by the creek in Marble,
>   Colorado.
> Our wolfdog from the time I was in utero, until fifth
>   grade.
> Her presence like a great warrior auntie.
>
> Thank you, Frea, for being in our clan when we needed
>   you the most.
> I feel her pack standing white, gray, and black.
> Their thick fur warming my heart and skin through
>   snowy Colorado winters.

Their large steamy tongues licking our wounds,
    encircling my mother and me,
filling in all the cracks of our family.

I saw the book *Women Who Run with the Wolves*
on my mom's bookshelf around the time Frea died.
Mom had to put her to sleep.
She was in a lot of pain from cancer.
Mom held her as her heart stopped beating.
I left school early that day to grieve.

Frea could jump a six-foot fence if she wanted to.
She tamed herself most days to be part of our woman-
    wilderness,
but she'd kill chickens any time they clucked through
    our yard.

I grabbed her tail when I was a baby,
and she bit my face, just missing my eye.
Left the mark of our clan.

Winter is coming.
I haven't rolled in the snow for over a decade.
In a wolf pack, I am warmed by running,
sledding, howling, belonging.
In cold moonlight, I find connection.
Frea taught us the ways of the clan.

THE FEMALE TIGERS by Katie Kindle

I ask my ancestors,
the female tigers of my birthright,
for strength and wisdom.

Wrap me in your golden body
of the sky's anguish.
I ask the hummingbird if it's warm.
It is all she has ever known.
Ask me if I am thirsty,
the succulent juice of the dripping mango
reminds me.

You know the answer, which you choose to ignore —
What should I do with all these leftover butterflies?
It is too hot, so we try to hide them, you reply:
We are only as safe as the sky.

We all fall down like the dancing leaves.
Some of us drown in the lake's sunset
or the dust of stars.

This urgency should make it easier.
I tried gardening to remake the future
but got lost in the hailstorm.
I ask you now
earth, sky, and fire:
Teach me to write.
Teach me to grow more time
from this knowledge.

Dancing with the Dark

Let's stay in this place of holy darkness for just a little while
longer as we learn to dance with it. What would it feel like to
have darkness reach for you, wrap its arms around you? Imagine being embraced by the dark as you begin to sway, until the

beat of your dark heart entrains, and you move together, free of fear, trusting your body, trusting your instincts, letting go of anything that holds you back, as you boogie effortlessly under the harvest moon.

Body/Mindfulness: Close your eyes and go inside. Let your breath find you and breathe you. Open to the darkness. Ask the dark for this dance. Imagine yourself dancing with this darkness. Be free to explore anything and everything that arises for you. What does it feel like to dance with the dark? Let the years, the sickness, the sadness, the loss, the exhaustion fall away as you dance with the dark as your partner.

WRITE NOW! *Write about your experience dancing with the darkness. How did you feel? How did you move? How did the darkness move? How did you find each other? What happened during this dark dance?*

Examples

DANCE WITH ME, DARKNESS by Liz Kughn

> Dance with me, darkness
> take me down your long path
> your deep well
> free me from myself
> and help me find my way.
>
> Walk with me into my emptiness,
> my not knowing enveloping me
> as I sink below the surface with one eye open
> and pen my deepest fears

embracing them finally
owning them without shame.

Stay with me as I sink
down into emptiness
like a buoy in uncharted waters
my own decay washing over me
begging the question —
who am I really?

I kiss the darkness
touching my lips to cold stone
wrapping my arms around
my own tenuous humanity.
I am tender
I am not who I think I am
and I am sorrow.
I name it with words
that set me free.

DARK DANCE by Hamidah Glasgow

Darkness

underneath all

                              before & after,
      light

my soul stirs
                              longing for more

Darkness

dark soup   bubbles of
air

nutrients of the four winds

No mind   no thought

no   thing

only   and

a continuous soul being

sparkles of stars

my flesh dissipates   my bones dissolve

nightmoon comfort me   with your dark lightness

before & after,   the end.

CHAPTER 9

Desire

Allow desire to be the compass pointing you home.

Desire is a touchy topic. Many of us have learned that desire is the cause of suffering. But is it desire or is it our attachment to the desire that causes suffering? Ah. For some of us desire is a compass pointing us home to what makes our heart hum. What if our desire were a deep intelligence within us, pulling us toward what we truly love? Of course, we can distinguish between the desire to eat a whole bar of chocolate and the desire to serve a worthy cause. It's the deeper desires I'm talking about, the ones that keep surfacing, poking their heads up like wild weeds, reaching out from inside us, knocking, whispering, whimpering, crying, yelling, screaming, whatever it takes to get our attention. These desires want us to wake up, remember what we love, connect with what makes us burn and sparkle with hope, creativity, and possibility. What if desire were the compass pointing us in the direction of what makes our heart sing?

Join me as we befriend our desire and open a line of communication by listening, the most sacred of all acts. We'll listen deeply to the voice within us that knows what we desire — what we love and yearn for. We're going to bring our desire into the light of our awareness, commune with it, build trust with it, celebrate it so it can guide us home to greater joy, fulfillment, vitality, and purpose.

When I Was a Child

The best way I know to get in touch with what we truly desire is to call up our inner child. By inviting the memories and sensations of what brought us pure joy and fulfillment as children, we can access our original blueprint, what we came here to do. We're going to tap into our inner child to learn about who we were before we were taught that desire was bad or selfish, before we were told what we should and should not want and who we could or could not be. Let's dig in and call up our childhood selves.

Body/Mindfulness: Close your peepers and snuggle in as we breathe our way back into our childhoods. Take a few deep breaths and travel back in time to a moment in your childhood when you felt whole, connected, happy, and free. Notice where you are and what you're doing. Give your attention to the details. Bask in that feeling. Let it fill you up.

WRITE NOW! *Write about a moment in your childhood when you felt whole, connected, happy, and free. What are you doing in this moment? Has any part of this experience informed your current life? My happy place as a kid was writing stories, singing, dancing, being in nature. I have made a life based on the very things that were my joys as a child. Notice if some aspect of your childhood experience of well-being still calls to you, something that brought you joy but got pushed away as you grew up. Explore this in your writing.*

Examples

WHEN I WAS A GIRL by Jac-Lynn Stark

When I was a girl
I loved to stand at
the crest of the hill outside
the rows of brick apartment buildings
and call in the wind
whenever I heard the
soft growl of thunder
somewhere not too far away
the tiny hairs on my arms
would tingle in the electric air
as I raised my arms toward
the darkening sky
and summoned the lightning
my face upward like a thirsty flower
my long brown hair wafting wild
away from my neck
I felt powerful
like some kind of goddess
who could make a storm happen
just by wishing it.

RUNNING BAREFOOT by Dawn Li

Running barefoot
across the top of the wall
laughing into the wind
the world passes me by —
a blur of green and yellow trees
red and brown houses.

I am six
I move like air
desire without desiring
play without wishing.

No key to the house, no problem
my little body finds a hole in the back
and I crawl in
no food, I light a fire
and cook sweet potatoes.

On sunny days
I watch light revealing colors
on the silkworms and goldfish
in my hands.

Heart Compass

The word *desire* derives from the Latin word for "star" (*sidus*), expressing a longing for direction and home. What if by the very act of desiring we orient ourselves, finding and following our star to a place of heart and home? What if desire, pleasure, and fulfillment are our compasses? What if our mission is to give ourselves what we truly desire to feel met, happy, and whole? What if a happy heart, mind, and body are our true purpose, our star?

Let's listen to our desires, from the smallest to the biggest, and see where they point us. Perhaps you desire rest, sleep, stillness, alone time, movement, exercise, touch, intimacy, connection, partnership, community, home, vacation, adventure, meaningful work or service, or creative self-expression.

Your desire is welcome here! What do you desire? What do you *really* desire?

Body/Mindfulness: Get cozy and close your eyes. Ride the waves of your breath as you soften and open, arriving in your inner world. Clear your mind and imagine you have a magic compass in your hand. This compass responds to your desire, which is connected to your love, enthusiasm, joy, and pleasure. Place your hand with the imaginary compass on your heart and breathe into the compass. Ask yourself, "What do I desire?" Let the compass whir and spin. Then drop in deeper by asking, "What do I *really* desire?" Watch the compass gain momentum and hum until it lands on the deep desire of your heart. When it does, you'll feel it ring like a bell. Acknowledge it and say thank you. Make a quick note if you need.

Next, place your hand with the compass on your belly. Breathe into the compass and ask yourself, "What do I desire? And then, what do I *really* desire?" Let the compass attune with the desire in your belly. When it lands on the answer, acknowledge it and say thank you. Make a note if you need.

Finally, place the hand with the compass on your womb or your vagina, breathing into the compass, asking yourself, "What do I desire? What do I *really* desire?" Let the compass vibrate and whirl until it dials into the true desire of your womb or vagina. When you have a clear answer, say thank you. Make a note if you need. Thank your compass and put it away somewhere safe so it will be there again when you want it.

WRITE NOW! *Write about your experience. What was it like working with your compass? What did you feel and learn? What did your compass and your body tell you about your desires? Give* *each area an opportunity to express its desire. Then respond to these desires with permission, welcoming, celebration, and gratitude. You can do this in sections — heart, belly, womb, and vagina — or you can weave them into one piece, one fine arrow pointing you home.*

Examples

THIS ARROW by Shankari Linda Barerra

> This arrow
> a black-edged
> brown feather
> with a white
> centered stripe
>
> clear as day
> twice as mysterious
>
> This compass points blue
> the whole large expanse
> of this luminous color
>
> Blue of sky
> and
> feather of wings
> the freedom
> of which
>
> unbinds
> my
> soul
> in flight

E
man
ci
pa
tion

this
sovereignty
liberates
my
deliverance

What more can I desire?

IF YOU DIED TODAY by Suzanne Jagers Neuweld

My heart desires to live each day as if it's my last ...

If you died today
would you be pleased with how you
chose to spend this day?
Or would you choose to follow
the list of tasks?

Would you walk among
nature's explosion of spring flowers
that may be here only today?

Or would you follow the lists,
that plan for tomorrow
that plan for next week
that plan for next year.

The chocolate lily,
California fetid adder's-tongue,

here for such a brief time in spring —
just like you.

One big rainstorm
one big wind
one human foot
can squash your beauty.

I choose the mountains
the colors and magic of flowers,
columbine, shooting stars,
checkers and narcissus,
all here so briefly.

We are all here so briefly.

Color Crazy

Understandably, many of us resist giving ourselves permission
to feel desire. After all, desire has been schooled and shamed
out of us. What if knowing and allowing our desire were as
natural as being drawn toward a color of our liking? Everyone
has a favorite color. What's yours? Ever wondered why you
favor that color? Why do we gravitate toward certain colors
and feel repelled by others? Color is vibration and frequency,
and we feel it and respond. We don't argue with ourselves
about liking a certain color, the way we might argue with ourselves about our desires. Some colors energize us, others calm
us; some make us feel safe, others make us feel sick. Often the
colors we resonate with change. Why is it that one day the
color you've been wearing for years suddenly doesn't feel right
anymore? The colors we vibe with give us insight about ourselves. I used to be a purple and turquoise girl. Now I'm peach

and terra-cotta. This speaks to me of a softening in myself.
What do your colors say about you? Knowing your desires can
be as easy as knowing your favorite color.

Body/Mindfulness: Close your eyes and go inside. Ride a few
cycles of breath as you arrive in your inner world. Place a hand
on your heart and a hand on your belly, and invite the color
of your desire. A few colors may sing and swirl through your
awareness, but you'll know your special color when it arrives.
You'll feel it. It will hum and buzz as though it's alive. It will
wrap you in its warmth or cool you with its freshness. Say yes to
this color. Let it fill you. Breathe this color in and out. It's simple, right? Remember this feeling of knowing your color, and
continue to draw on this knowing. What's your color?

WRITE NOW! *Write about your color. Describe, invoke, associate, sing about, and riff on the color of your desire. Why this
color? How this color? When and where this color? What means
this color? Write everything that comes to mind when you allow
yourself to be enveloped and immersed in the color of your desire.
For extra fun, remove the name of the color everywhere from your
poem after you write it, except for the title, no matter how non-
sensical it makes your poem sound. Read your poem aloud with
gusto. Own this color!*

Examples

DARK PURPLE by Geneva Toland

> you are the color of pleasure
> the lust that lingers
> in the doorway
> where lovers meet

licking the chocolate, melted
from edge of plate
you smile a secret
meant for me alone

often overlooked, you
the moment just before
the black night claims sky, you
the lady's slipper crawling out of
the hot dark, you
the last leaf to burst into flame

i covet you, condemn you, cherish you,
how could i not?

the spells you weave
are ribboned around my wrists
gladly, i follow your supple steps
into the dark garden

lay me down where the roses
have bloomed and died,
let the thorns graze my skin
oh, let me be eaten!

you, the nymph i have
searched the forests for
take me back,
teach me to turn my hair to snakes
my fingers to flowers
how to arch my back up until
i can etch my spine along the sky
and lick the stars

you are not the end
the last sip tipped from the bottle

no, you are the moment
before the beginning
the kiss before the kiss
the lips before the word
the hand before the brush of skin

you, the deepest of purples
how long i've waited for the fullness
of your hips to rise
into mountains.

RUST by Korynn Amm

Rust, you old soul,
how you've held it all together as your tires beat the road
exhausted in your wisdom as you let it all unfold
within the cracks, tiny glimpses of the stories that you
        told
from the routes around the desert, searching for the
        waterfall
and the sunrise on the days when you believed you had
        it all
inside you're gripping the glory as the years go passing by
you became another story as the ravens blinked their eyes
whispering to each other as they lay your feathers down
as they land upon the soil and settle softly on the ground
sinking deeper into seeds as you speak between the leaves
within the wind, you say, "I love you"
I love the incandescence of your skin as you ignite in me
        a light

I love the way you breathe in this warrior's breath,
    releasing this inner fight
for me to love a little deeper and still softening inside
I love the wisdom of the rust
inside the cracks, I realize —
I LOVE.

My Favorite Things

You know the song from *The Sound of Music*, right? And the hook, "these are a few of my favorite things"? Let's use this tune as a template as we learn to name and claim our desires, what makes us happy, what makes our heart sing. This feeling puts us in tune with ourselves, literally and metaphorically.

Body/Mindfulness: Close your beautiful eyes and ride the tides of your breath. Soften and open as you let go of the outside world and arrive inside yourself. Call up all the things that bring you joy, peace, a sense of connection and belonging, from the smallest joys to the biggest dreams, just like in the song, "raindrops on roses and whiskers on kittens." Name all the things that make your heart sing.

WRITE NOW! *Make a list of ten to twenty of your favorite things. Things that make you happy. Things you desire. Things that make your heart sing. For fun try singing to the tune of "My Favorite Things." Don't worry about it rhyming. Just sing out about the things that put you in tune with your desire. Here's the crazy part: when we allow ourselves our desires, we fall in love with life and we fall in love with ourselves. So write a piece about owning your desires and why you're worth falling in love with! Why should* *anyone love a woman who knows what makes her happy? Well, I trust you know the answer to that one! Give your piece a title like "Fall in Love with a Woman Who..." or "Fall in Love with This Woman..." or "I Fall in Love with Myself When..." Find your own way of saying it.*

Examples

IF YOU FALL IN LOVE WITH THIS WOMAN ...
by Mireya Quirie

If you fall in love with this woman
who craves a one-match campfire
and all that singing and dreamtalk
and laughter and healing that happens around it.
A woman who longs to inhale her children each night
and awaits their dreamlaughter.
A woman who gets giddy while packing her backpack
and positively skips through the airport.
A woman who swoons at her own cooking
who traps you in long discourses on her favorite fiction.
Who can chat lightweight backpacking gear
All. Night. Long.
A woman whose eyes sparkle with strangers soon to be
     friends.
A woman who needs, yes, needs, the sunset to set her
     right.
A woman who laughs out loud simply because she is on
     her bike
with a song in her ears.
A woman who longs for the opposite of a wall
and aches when too much time has passed
since her last journey to the middle of nowhere

with the stars exploding overhead
and her thighs cannot stand up for even one more
      moment
as she stirs her soup and inhales everything.
A woman whose eyes well up with tears
when she crests the hill —
in Santa Cruz, in Mendocino, in San Francisco
and sees Mama Ocean
as if they've been separated from each other for years.
Yes, if you fall in love with this woman,
know you will never be the same,
nor will you want to be.

WHEN YOU FALL IN LOVE WITH THIS WOMAN ...
by Nicole Phillips

A woman who feels when the rain is coming in her bones
and sings you a tearful storm prelude.
A woman who feels connected to earth and sky
and dances between them wholehearted and full-bodied.
A woman who welcomes the cyclical rhythms
of light and dark as constant as the earth does.
A woman who notices the colors
of other people's feelings and reflects them back.
A woman who writes, dances poetry, sings songs, chants
      into the darkness
and morning light, communes with ancestors, and
      drinks hot lemon water.
A woman who spins in the sand, arms outstretched,
drinking ocean mist through all her tendrils.
A woman who will leave if you hurt her
and stay if you love yourself.

A woman who is funny and full, who teaches and heals,
and who is honest with herself.
When you fall in love with this woman,
be ready to grow.
She will break you open, inspire you to live fully
and to stand tall in your own skin and bones.

Spirit Animal

In my workshops we often work with spirit animals, who help
us tune in to our deeper instincts and touch our wild knowing.
By the time you've taken a few of my workshops or written
your way through this book, you'll have a whole council of
animal guides you can call on for wisdom and companionship. Animals don't doubt their desires or their instincts. For
animals, desire is healthy. It helps them survive and thrive.
Today you will become a wild spirit animal, instinctual, sensual, savvy. Let's journey to sniff out which animal you need
to become at this moment, pointing you in the direction of
your desire.

Body/Mindfulness: Get comfy. Close your wild eyes. Feel
supported by what's underneath and behind you. Allow your
breath to breathe you. Invite your body to soften and open.
Put a hand on your heart and a hand on your belly. Arrive in
your inner world. For this invitation, we will become our own
spirit animal. Now, without thinking yourself there but rather
allowing your intuition and deep psyche to guide you, invite
yourself to become a wild animal. What animal might you be?
What animal-knowing would best serve you on this quest of
desire? You may find that a few animals inhabit you before you
know which one feels right. Stay with it. Trust yourself. When

you and your animal have chosen each other and it feels like a good fit, say hello. Be curious. Feel your body. Look out from your animal eyes. Sniff the air. Listen to the sounds around you. Sense your environment. You are in tune with your needs and desires. You trust your instincts. You are in a state of equanimity. You shake off what no longer serves you. When you get wounded, you rest and heal. You eat when hungry and sleep when tired. You live by the rhythms of nature. You find belonging with your pack. You're in tune with life. You follow your heart-knowing and your body-knowing. What animal are you?

WRITE NOW! *Write about what it's like to be this animal. How do you feel? What's your experience? What skills and wisdom do you bring as this animal? What's it like to feel connected to your instinct and your wild nature? As this animal, how do you know and meet your desire?*

Examples

I AM MOON RABBIT by Dawn Li

> My breath translucent
> my fur responding to every motion in the wind
> my footsteps feathers touching the earth
> my fluffy ears, antennae, turning like orbs,
> attuning to cosmic energy.
>
> Call me Moon Rabbit, the celestial one
> who took the longevity pill of her husband
> and flew to the moon eons ago.

I shine light into the world's darkest and most brutal
   corners.
I invite all sentient beings to become poets and lovers of
   the night.
Come adore one another.
Enact a forever song of blend and blood, time and tide.

Oh, gentle souls of the world,
have you seen the luminous me
on the entrance steps of your home
or under the jade tree
or sitting on the moon when it's full at night?

BEES by Jeannie McKenzie

We desire oneness
the magic of weaving
hum hive kinship with flowers.
This song we sing together
one voice harmonizing
with the magnetic lines
of earth and sky.

Patterns
geometries
holding us
in our luminous
hexagonal
holy homes.

We are blossom made
golden radiance

flying songs
of color.

Each flower-being
its own story
its own exuberance
scintillating
and true.

We carry the golden coins of pollen
the currency among us
the hum
thrum
buzz.

This music carries us
from one magnificent flower
to the next
as we ride the currents
of radiant melodies
deep pulsing
chords uplifting
luminous intertwining
color and sound
soaring the symphony
of wholeness.

CHAPTER 10

Bloom

Explore your life cycles,
from seed to bloom and back again.

Out of the dark, we bloom. Rest engenders renewal. Death births new life. Cycles. Again and again. Let's explore the cycle of fruition, the blooming. Right now, where I live in Northern California, it's springtime. Life is bursting open after winter's hibernation. I feel this in my body. I unfurl from my cocoon, stretch, and make my way outside into the sunshine. I follow my nose into the garden, where the jasmine is opening the fingers of her petals. Life has returned. I think about all the things I have seeded and grown in myself during this long winter. Patience, perseverance, kindness, new friends, new home, new book, new skills. How about you? What seeds are germinating in your life, ready to sprout and bloom?

How Does Your Garden Grow?

What's sprouting or blooming in your garden right now? Perhaps you've planted seeds of self-acceptance, compassion, curiosity, forgiveness, gratitude, creativity, health, alone time, rest, sleep, relationship, family, project, work, service, or community, to name just a few. Now is the time to water and weed. How does your garden grow?

Body/Mindfulness: Close your eyes and go inside. Find your breath and ride the tides in and out. Allow your body to soften and open. In your mind's eye, imagine a garden. See this garden as your life. What have you planted here recently, or what would you like to plant in terms of qualities, ways of being, lifestyle, new projects, new direction? Now imagine spring as a magical and spirited being come to help tend your garden. Work along with this being to get a sense of who they are, then thank them, and ask if you can call on them again.

WRITE NOW! *Make a quick list of what's growing in your garden. Then describe the magical being who arrives to help you. What do you notice about their energy? What do they look like? What do they wear? What do they say to you? My magical garden helper looks like Pippi Longstocking, has a wonderful sense of humor, and always brings me presents. Does yours bring you gifts? What are you growing in your garden, and how does this magical being help your garden grow? Write in second person,* you, *or third person,* he/she/they.

Examples

SPRING by Dawn Li

> Spring arrives,
> artist and healer
> born of bitter north wind.

With her new brushes,
she drizzles misty rain
upon earth's canvas,
painting treetops and grounds
the greens, reds, and oranges
of seasonal murals.

Quietly she sneaks in
through a little crack in the window
of my red thatched house
under a snowcapped mount.

She sends dew on my breath,
deepening my inhales and exhales
my eyes open wide with a smile —
Finally!

I walk out my door
and stand tall on the bridge
over the mountain stream
stretching —
my stiff spine,
forgotten arms,
shaky legs
from long winter days.

She warms each and every cell —
my limbs and muscles,
fluids and bones,
my meridians.

Now the grass, squirrels, birds,
and me, we are all singing,

even the daffodils bow their heads
in gratitude.

SPRING by Jeannie McKenzie

Spring, you never wear the same dress twice!
You pop up in daffodils then change your outfit to tulips
in a blink of an eye.

You swirl around in a tantrum
blowing off the tops of trees, whipping up dust storms
leaving behind a blanket of snow.

You make amends with your fragrant, frilly cloaks

Cherry
  Pear
      Apricot
        Peach

Each blossoming in succession.

Then you knock those blossoms to the ground in a
    downpour
wipe the slate clean, gaily scattering rainbows across the
    sky
and then, your offering — the most tender green shoots.

With you, my friend, everything is precious
and nothing is forever.

You teach me the elusive art of letting go
reminding me to fully appreciate
this ever-changing moment.

You open my heart wide and joyous
with each sprouting and snapping
you remind me of the boundless infinity
of creativity.

Dirt

No dirt, no garden. The success of a garden depends on its dirt. But what exactly is dirt? It's actually millions of micro-organisms. Dirt is a living being, and in nature, nothing is ever wasted. Every garden grows from the decay of what came before it. Dirt does the dirty alchemical work of turning the old into the new. Let's join the great work of the dirt. Consider what you can let go of that is dead and decaying, and return it to the dirt to be composted and made anew.

Body/Mindfulness: Close your eyes, get comfy, arrive. Allow yourself to be breathed, in and out, as your body softens and loosens. Turn your attention toward your inner dirt, and with kind curiosity, get down in that dirt on your hands and knees and delight in your dirt-caked nails and dirt-stained knees as you inquire about what you're ready to let go and turn to compost.

WRITE NOW! *Write two lists, one exploring what you're ready to let go of and the other describing what you want to plant. Write five to ten of each. Be as specific as possible about what you're feeding to the compost pile and what you're planting this season.*

Examples

RHYTHMS OF DIRT by Ann McGuire

> I grab the shovel and bury the voices that have held me
> > back
> and almost had their way with me.
>
> I send them deep into the earth,
> > where their screams only wake the worms.
>
> They turn and churn,
> > in cacophony.
>
> Until they break into slender strings of sound,
> anger and resentment swallowed by deep, cool earth.
>
> The strings twirl and rise upward,
> > pushed to the surface by ageless rhythms of dirt.
>
> Ready to accept the message I choose to plant,
> I am here and ready to grow my song.

DIRT by Verana Bailowitz

> Please do not wait any longer.
> Swallow me into your sludge.
> I'm done. I give up.
>
> I go now, with hawk wings and freckled breasts.
> I go with mud squeezing between my toes,
> each step steady.

I climb slowly, through your layers of rich chocolate,
fuzzy walnut, and caramelized onion,
a juicy, steamy stew.

I bellow and bow, my forehead to the earth,
dust on my brow,
the only crown I've ever wanted to wear.

Take me into your belly, strip me bare.
Take me into your dark soil, your heat, your rot.
Bury me up to my nostrils. Put me with the worms.

Cover my eyes with your dark weight.
Eat all that is ripe to decay and return.

In you, I am absorbed and renewed.
In you, I become what I am.

Bloomers

Forgive me, I couldn't resist. When I was dreaming up ideas
for this section, the word *bloomers* popped up in my mind like
a wild California poppy. And I said yes! It made me laugh.
Bloomers! You know, those things we wear under our skirts?!
We've all got a panty tale, a best or worst pair story, a good,
bad, naughty, embarrassing, or sexy undie anecdote.

Body/Mindfulness: Settle in and close your eyes. Breathe
your way into your inner garden. When you're cozy, call up a
memory about your bloomers, your favorite or least favorite
pair, a crazy underwear story. Dig up all the juicy details.

WRITE NOW! *Write an ode to your bloomers, to your best or worst pair, to your lacy or frilly ones, to your sexy fantasy pair. Write a funny undie story, about going commando, or any other tale you're ready to tell or invent about your bloomers. And hey, for fun, which ones are you wearing right now? Who, me? Purple cheeky boy shorts!*

Examples

BLOOMERS by Meredith Heller

> I washed each pair
> with Dr. Bronner's
> lavender castile soap
> in a bucket
> with river water.
>
> I scrubbed
> and I swished
> and I made sure
> there were lots
> of bubbles.
>
> I rinsed their thin skins
> thoroughly wringing out
> the old ghosts
> from their cotton crotches
> and lace trim.
>
> I hung each frillery
> on a length of string
> I'd strung between two trees
> bordering my campsite.

Each pair draped gingerly
over the line —
purple lace boy shorts
tiger-striped bikini
black-and-white tie-dye hipster
hot-pink thong.

I have to admit,
they were beautiful creatures
each one dangling there
swinging its legs
nickering its own little story
after having nestled
my most intimate parts.

I sit on the big rock
to admire my clean tribe
of dainties with a smile
on my face and I think,
now this is *my* kind
of prayer flag.

Incantations stained
into silken skin
my signature
inscribed in sighs.

Panty prayers
wind scribbling
dream flowers
across pretty petals.

The elements eating
away their karma
rejoicing their secrets
and their sins
as they remember
how to sing.

GARDEN VARIETY by Jac-Lynn Stark

Our faces bright on the Zoom screen
like petals of a glorious flower
we talk about our underwear
each of us sharing what color and material
we chose today to skim over our butts
and nestle against those more private parts.

Like our faces,
our undies are a garden of variety
demure beige under white pants
polka dots dancing in the dark
playful boy shorts or high-cut legs
fancy lace embroidered ones
bamboo by Boody
or even absolutely nothing.

My own today are more colorful
than what I usually wear
bright-green-and-blue paisley designs
twirl and pirouette around
my pussy and ass
the most colorful pair I own.

My undies, like too much in my life,
lean too far toward the practical

just do the job, cover me up
elastics stretched out
or ripped away from the cloth
faded cotton soft and comfy
but also shabby and worn
this collection stunted by benign neglect.

It's time to go shopping
for my own bright garden
of playful colors and wild prints
to light a little spark under my jeans
and tease out a secret inner smile
both above and below.

BEIGE PANTIES by Teddi Dysart

Today is beige.
Surprisingly, a color of vast emotion,
practical, nondescript, serious
in its beigeness. Stoic.
Not to be messed with.

I have more beige
than frilly magenta,
heavy black,
stark white,
or frivolous cheetah print.
Beige is the color that chooses itself.

Coyote beige traipsing stealthily
through tall crinkling grass,
running, trying not to be noticed
by the world

as she forages and dances,
calling to the moon,
wearing her protective coat
of beige.

Blossoming

What does blossoming feel like for you? For me it's that feeling of warmth and opening, of unfurling, flowering, billowing, rippling, surging, exploding, emerging. Let's explore some experiences that feel like blossoming. Consider dancing, swimming, laughing, painting, playing music, having an orgasm; the first swallow of wine or that first bite of food when you're hungry. Or perhaps you can find something related to blossoming such as a shooting star, a rainstorm, a sunrise or sunset, a music concert. What expresses the feeling of blossoming for you?

Body/Mindfulness: Cozy in, close your eyes, and arrive. Petal open with your breath. Imagine what blossoming feels like to a flower. Bring this feeling into your body and heart. Feel yourself opening, petal by petal. Breathe yourself into blossoming. You know this feeling? Now try associating it with something you like to do such as singing, dancing, painting, writing, exercising, making love. Fill yourself with this feeling.

WRITE NOW! *Write about what blossoming feels like for you. Do you burst open in celebration, or do you unfurl slowly, petal by prayerful petal? Try comparing the feeling of blossoming to an experience you associate with this feeling, such as sailing or* *dancing. Name it and describe it. Once you've written your piece, go back and cross out all the places where you name the experience so that all you're left with are the words describing the experience of blossoming. For example, instead of saying "the rainstorm started slowly and built until it thundered down" just say "started slowly, built, thundered." This practice evokes the experience, and we become part of the blossoming.*

Examples

SAILING by Mireya Quirie

> The sky is vast and forever
> cerulean-blue
> dizzying depth
> and my boat rocks gently
> as the water laps
> against the slick shoreline
> licking gently.
> His weathered hands touch the boat's sides,
> mast, halyard, transom, and tiller,
> the boom.
> His calloused fingers glide over each part
> with a love that comes from knowing her for a lifetime.
> She yawns, she inhales,
> she stretches, shivers,
> her shoulders straighten,
> her spine hunches and arches,
> she reaches upward.
> And then, and then,
> she catches the breeze's tickle.
> Giggle, flap, wave
> she undulates, hungry

deep inside she remembers
this is wind, this is sky, this is water.
She stretches from tip to tip
along the mast, along the boom
taut, jaunty, ready for adventure,
giddy with the unknowing.

AURORA BLOOMS by Dawn Li

shivering
florets of light
gently, resolutely
spread open the oppressive
blankets of darkness

threads of gold and red
rolling in
colors splashing
in the ocean sky
east of celestial ceiling

a fireball
climbs out
tearing apart
layers and layers
of blinds

blissful
a figure
stands in
the far horizon
the ribbons of her dress

flying
lotus patterns
lit bright
by the sun
aaaaaaah

the ribbons
lift the figure
across the sky
she loops around and around
diffusing herself

her light blossoms
fall through the air
tirelessly
until darkness
engulfs her

with a long sigh,
she chooses
to return
aurora
blooms.

Group Bloom

If you do this writing invitation with a group, it's fun to forage a couple of juicy lines from each person's poem to create a group bloom.

GROUP BLOOM

rooted surrender
snug embrace
satiated softening

ache
cheery spring-lipped song
surrender
exhale
flesh from my bones
make music with myself
lifted and drifted
fast and forever
cerulean dizzying
licking gently
humming
unfurling
salt shivers
arching giggle
undulate
hungry bursting
reach the sun
push through the earth
fits and starts
my green stem spine
thrusting
birth canal
shedding
not ready, not steady
jumped from the moon
flowering cocoon.

Soul Flower

You've worked hard, turning, building, and seeding the soil of your heart to usher in your next bloom, your special soul flower. Let her be as big, beautiful, and wild as you can dream up or as gentle, tender, and fragile as you desire. This is your soul, your flower. Do you wake early to catch the dew? Are you night-blooming? Do you enchant and dazzle, or are you subtle and sweet? Are your petals a velvety jewel tone, or are you a dainty pale beauty? How do you bloom?

Body/Mindfulness: Close the petals of your eyes and go deep inside. Place a hand on your heart and a hand on your belly. Breathe into your soul soil. Imagine that when you were born, you were given a magic seed to plant at the right moment. Now is the moment. Go ahead and push the seed gently into the soil of your heart with your finger. Trust that it will germinate and grow with the sun and rain of your love. Imagine this seed bursting open and sprouting. Feel its roots, your roots, burrowing deep in the earth. Feel the earth holding you. Inhale and pull nutrients up from the soil, up your green stem spine, and into your blossoming heart. Exhale and bloom open. Breathe yourself through a few rounds of gathering nutrients and blossoming open. Experience yourself as you grow and bloom into your full soul flower with the unique essence you came here to share.

WRITE NOW! *Describe your soul flower. What kind of bloom are you? What do you look like? What do we call you? Where do you grow? What does it feel like to be you? What magic and medicine do you bring to the world?*

Examples

BLOSSOM OF INFINITE CHANGE by Karen Burt-Imira

> Call me *Asantameenhah-Amoonichi*
> I am the flower of evolution

and infinite change.
No static thing can know me
only in fluid continual movement
do I exist,
infinite motion.

I am the color of sunlight traversing
a raindrop prisming into kindred hues
with each new curving angle,
crimson to gold
brightest of greens to cobalt-blue
indigo to black with the night,
infinite translucence.

I sing out with golden mellifluous tones
underground tunneling bass moans
soft white chocolate whistling sweetness
bright darting hummingbird whirring,
infinite translations.

My fragrance is a grass field
after a thunderstorm
sliding into delight,
float worthy and gleeful
then strong penetrating,
standing stock-still
and finally, drifting planets
gone out of orbit for the day,
infinite transiting.

My petals are velveteen
then silken, wooly, lacy

thickly firm and supple
my pistils on blue stems are topped
with a shower of waving filaments
that rise into red stalks
topped by sticky spring-green balls
and, finally, a wholesome black hole
rimmed by yellow strands,
infinite transformations.

My pollen-coated stamens
stand in a circle of grace
a flurry of rows
a marching band in single file
splashing powder-blue then mandarin-orange
then angel-white, and earth-brown promises,
infinite transpiration.
Call me *Asantameenhah-Amoonichi*,
flower of infinite evolution.

BIRTHDAY BLOOM by Verana Bailowitz

My roots are wide and strong
sometimes twisting, always
stretching, sliding their way
through open pockets
of moisture and nourishment.

My stem is made of strength and courage
covered in fine crystal dew
breathing life, pulsing breezes
humming rhythmic hymns
my hips swaying
with all pains, triumphs, loves.

My leaves are curious
unfurling to touch time
wrapping around me
in protection as I grow
full and fearless.
And my bloom!
She climbs and curls and twists
breathing herself open, slowly at first,
her inhale, an invitation.

If you come close and look inside
you find a cove of treasure, a single pearl
sanded and smoothed from lifetimes
of tears and betrayals, loneliness and love.
Irritated and polished into a round sparkling center
dipped in the healing honeys of promise,
of love.

CHAPTER 11

Zen Bones

Boil your poems down to the essence.

Nature is my temple. I spend my summers camping and writing beside rivers and oceans, immersing myself in nature to remember to slow down, attune to earth's rhythms, and find the metaphors in nature that teach me how to be human. For the past handful of summers, I've camped beside my favorite river in Northern California. Last year I fell so deeply in love, I married the river. There is something alchemical that happens for me when I live outside, woven into the elements. It puts me in a Zen state, peels me down to the essence, helps me remember who I am and what matters. Come along with me now and commune with nature. Touch the essence of who you are, bone-deep. Together we'll discover the metaphors in nature that help weave us back into the great web of life.

Why Zen bones? My workshops are geared toward generative writing rather than deep-dive editing, but my students asked for practice editing. So to bone up on our editing skills, I added another layer of metaphor by making this section a practice in boiling not only ourselves but also our poems down to the essence, down to the shining bones.

For this writing journey, give yourself time and space after each piece you write to practice editing down to the bones, what my students refer to as "Zen-boning" a piece. Please be kind with yourself when cutting away extra flesh and connective tissue. Keep all your drafts. Try a few versions. Remember, this is not a poem *perfect*, it's a poem *practice*.

Zen-Boning Guidelines

- What is the essence, the bones, of this piece?
- Which lines are the keepers — the most vivid, rich, juicy, fresh, chewy, singing, shining, raw, potent, poignant, evocative, moving, emotional, original, wow lines?
- Which lines can you boil out so all that remains are the shining bones?

Trees

Think roots, trunk, branches, leaves, blooms, fruit, seeds. The living cycle of a tree is extraordinary. Contained within the seed is the whole tree. Through their xylem and phloem, trees pull nutrients up from the soil to feed their highest leaves and branches. Through photosynthesis, they absorb carbon dioxide and produce oxygen. We should all be students of trees, sitting at the base of their trunks and communing with them until we remember how to live in harmonious reciprocity with each other and the earth. What can we learn about ourselves from trees? I asked a little boy I once met at the river what he wants to be when he grows up, and he said, "A tree." Me too.

Body/Mindfulness: Go outside if possible; otherwise, look out your window. Find a tree that calls to you. Maybe it's tall or gnarled, weeping or fruiting. You'll know your tree when you see it. Go sit at its feet, its base, its roots. Close your eyes and breathe yourself in tune with this tree. Feel its life force. Use your senses to discover the beauty and wisdom of this tree-being. What do you experience in its presence? What does it teach you about how to live in deeper harmony with yourself and the world?

WRITE NOW! *Write about how it feels to commune with your tree. Describe this tree. What does it look like, where does it live, what season of growth is it currently in? What moves you about this tree? Why did this tree call to you? Can you relate to this tree? What do you learn about yourself and life from this tree?*

Examples

CIRCLE OF SEVEN by Jo Walker

> As a sma' wee human of sapling proportions, I decide that one day I'll have a garden, and in my garden is a circle of trees, maple and oak, a circle of seven. I dance in my circle of trees because they hold a loving space for me. I call them my Standing Ones, great, tall, magnificent. They are happy to be here with me, and I am delighted that the Great Gardener who planted them thought kindly of me, knowing that I need my trees to love me, as only good, kindly guardians can. I tend to my circle of seven. I dance and sing for them. I hug and hold them. The Fae and the Elfin dance too, and the river gurgles its way into the deep roots half a kilometer east when the leaves fall in autumn blessings. I kiss each one and name them, before the ceremonial burning. I smoke scry and send songs to the stars upon the billowing smoke signals. In the night my trees become

Ents; the Fae have cast a spell upon their roots and they dance with me. Their branches bend, scoop, and cradle me. They twirl and squeeze me until I giggle-snort, and in the morning I awaken to find each one has swapped places with the next, and I have come alive with twigs twisted in my hair and a tiny strong waist from having danced all day and twirled all night. My circle of trees teach me when to be still and when to be vibrant. My friends, my Standing Ones, between us there is only tenderness and deep respect, and although we are a different species, we understand one another because we dance together in the language of love.

FAITH & FOG by Karen Burt-Imira

Expecting hard crusty armor
I touch redwood's bark
but this gentle giant's
thick auburn skin
is wet and spongy
with a soft push,
an easy imprint.
She harvests the fog
absorbent and receptive
she drinks its sustenance
imbibes its mysterious offering.
I too will drink the mystery.

Moon

Think moon, feel moon. Grandmother moon, harvest moon, hunter moon. Waxing, waning, new and full moon. Crescent moon. Gibbous moon. Blue moon. Dark side of the moon. Lunar eclipse. Blood moon. Lunatic. Moon time. Twenty-eight-day cycle of menses and moon. Women and moon are inseparable. Moon is our mirror, our mother, our partner, the bane of our blues and the elixir of our midnight dances with our muse. Let's commune with the moon as she circle-dances around the earth.

Body/Mindfulness: Go outside if possible; otherwise, look out your window at the moon. It can be a daytime or a nighttime moon. Any phase will do. There is always magic associated with the moon. Gaze at the moon and bask in her beauty. What do you see and feel? Are you in tune with the moon? Can you relate to her cycles of empty and full, dark and luminous?

WRITE NOW!   *Write about your experience with the moon. What phase is she in? Does the moon influence your mood? What does the moon symbolize for you? Do you have a moon ritual or ceremony? Would you like to invent one? I know people who leave a bowl of water out under a full moon and drink it in the morning to recharge them. How do you commune with the moon?*

Examples

TOASTING THE MOON by Jac-Lynn Stark

> Two nights ago I watched the almost
> full moon rise behind pine trees in Maine
> sitting in one of the striped chairs
> I bought when we were new
> I sipped cheap red wine

from a blue enamel coffee cup
while inside the dark tent
you muttered in your sleep.

I toasted the moon
watched it climb the branches
toward the tops of the trees
its brilliance striped with scattered shadows
breaking into segments like old puzzle pieces
that don't quite interlock the way they used to
corners blunted, edges curled from dampness and age.

You and I have seen many phases together
the blank sky of the new moon
the slivers of white growing bigger each night
the luminous roundness of the ripe moon
and then the shrinking back toward nothing.
Like the moon, we have gone through changes —
from lovers, to a couple, to estrangement, to friendship.

A few days earlier I reveled in
the touch of someone new
not knowing whether this would
grow full and ripe
or pass like a meteor
that lights up the sky
brilliant and fleeting —
yet still beautiful.

GRANDMOTHER MOON by Verana Bailowitz

Last night I emptied
the belly of my golden grief

into the warm palms
of deep desert valleys.

The tears have been stirring,
preparing, pulsing for days
beneath the surface
of smiles and moving-right-alongs
stretched too tight across me.

Grief lurks. Grief waits.
Waits for the moment
when everything is safe enough
for the most natural thing to happen
on the heels of loss.

Last night I erupted
in hot molten tears,
stars exploding,
snot waves crashing over,
upon my soft cheeks.
It is time.
The wind whips.
My open palms glow.
My grandmother is everywhere.
My tears break down doors
holding any sense of me together.
Tremors of gratitude.
Roofless. Ruthless.
In unabashed release,
undulating catharsis.

My grandmother humming
in my ears.

Last night my tears turned
the new moon full.
I emptied myself
into my grandmother's hands,
my tears filling her womb.

I crawl inside
and let go
into this next life.

Wild Crossing

Today we'll work with wild animal allies, but don't go dreaming up the royals: eagles, elephants, tigers, and bears. Instead, look to a humble wild one who has recently crossed your path. For example, at the river this week I saw a bullfrog, a turtle, a snake, an osprey, a muskrat, a mama duck and her nine ducklings, bumblebees, and dragonflies. Each had a message for me. Perhaps around your home, in your garden, or out on your daily walk you crossed paths with a wild one. Butterfly, honeybee, blue jay, hawk. Owl, fox, salamander, snake. Raven, deer, beetle, spider. Watch this wild one for as long as they allow, and gather the message, metaphor, and medicine this creature brings you. Thank them for their wild crossing.

Body/Mindfulness: Go outside and look around your home to spy a wild creature crossing your path. It could be rare like an owl or fox, or as common as an ant. Say hello. Commune with it for as long as it allows. Does it notice you? What's its MO? How does it navigate life? Can you relate in any way? What message does this wild one offer you?

WRITE NOW!   *Write about the wild one who crossed your path. Where did you see them? How do they move? In what ways do they mirror or provide metaphor at this moment? What do you learn from them?*

Examples

CATERPILLAR GIRL by Meredith Heller

> She is one of those young women
> with a sunflower face
> a heart full of honey
> eyes scooped from the river.
>
> She swings through her days
> in a red silk slip
> that kisses her knees
> and plunges at the neck
> revealing the soft curve
> of her breast.
>
> And there, along the edge
> of her hem, a caterpillar,
> suddenly, thick as your thumb
> prehistoric, with red-tipped horns,
> crawling up her dress.
>
> Oh! she yelps, not sure yet
> if she feels afraid or blessed
> when her ocean-eyed lover asks,
> scared? Nah, she laughs
> and settles in,
> curious and content.

We chitchat about camping
and traveling
and the possibility of Yosemite
and all the while
this caterpillar climbs
with its multitude
of wrought-iron legs
up her body
finally nestling
in the hair
atop her head.

We joke about it
spinning a cocoon
that will hang
from her ear
like a silken dangle.

She'll sleep sitting up
for weeks, in service
to its birthing
and one fine day
it will emerge.

After having turned to goo
melting and metabolizing
each and every molecule
into imaginal cells
that dream themselves anew,
winged and wild
and ready
to fly.

JELLYFISH by Nicole Phillips

    Underwater
    you billow
    lithe tentacles

    Elegant diaphragms
    weightless in darkness
    dance the breath of sea

    July at the beach
    you bubble in tide pools
    you dry up on hot sand

    Globby and oval
    as my embryo
    in the tub

    One year ago
    remnants of my
    fertile wish

    Your glassy goo shimmers
    under afternoon sunlight
    shined up by a year

    Of floating in saltwater tears
    washed up on land.
    Jellyfish, show me

    how you dance.

SNAKE FRIEND by Jessica Ulrich

Tope and I met by surprise
she snakes quietly into my loving heart
curls her soft body tightly in a chamber
providing me warmth and understanding.

Staring into each other's eyes
we share a special moment
words are not needed
our hearts bond as one.

Honestly, I never cared for snakes
yet Tope is beautiful and calm
unlike any ordinary snake;
I want to be friends forever.

She offers me a small gift box
pink with a glorious white bow
inside I find a gold heart locket
I notice there is no photo within.

She shares a story with me
and I listen closely to every word:
"We need time for ourselves."
She chants this phrase twice.

Self-love, her gift for me today
exactly what I need to hear.
I need time for myself,
only then can I help others.

Water

Water equals life. Water is sacred. Our bodies are 80 percent water. We *are* water. We say someone is worth their salt, but I wonder if it might be more accurate to say that someone is worth their water. Find some water to commune with. A stream, a river, the ocean; bathwater, dishwater, pool water, a tall glass of water. For those of us who live where water comes out of pipes in our homes, take a moment and give thanks, and then consider how sacred every drop of water is for people who walk miles to gather it and carry it home. Water is life.

Body/Mindfulness: Go outside, if possible, to any body of water, the ocean, a river, a creek, rain, if you're lucky. Or take a bath, wash the dishes, wash your car, water your plants. Do something that allows you to engage with water. Notice how you feel. What does water evoke in you?

WRITE NOW! *Write about your experience with water. What kind of water, and where? Was it still or moving? Did you simply witness it, or did you engage with it somehow? How does this water reflect your nature? What medicine or metaphor does this water offer you?*

Examples

WATER PRAYER by Mireya Quirie

> My feet at the water's edge
> my toes giggling as waves come up to kiss them.
> This is home.
> I look out to the horizon, and I'm held.

Only then can I take it all off.
Me, a weary knight, my crying unheard inside my armor.
First, I lay down my lance,
century-old sand nibbles its sharp edge.
Next the helmet, as my ears rush and crash
with lapping waves, birdcall, the song buried in my throat.
Finally, I drop the chain mail constricting my chest
and I gasp, gulping sea and sky.
Thank you, I laugh-cry, as her salty water pours from my
    eyes.
Absorbing, releasing, absorbing, releasing,
in tides, until my soul is cleansed
and I could float away pure and soaring.

I have felt her waves
carving, lapping, pounding, crashing.
Her power and her caress, the same
as she holds me, fiercely protective, all-knowing
and forgives my every drop of self-doubt.

I stumble over words of gratitude,
desperate pleas for help,
joyful songs of praise,
all fuse and combust,
rocketing skyward
toward the horizon
as I join the sunset,
bowing in prayer.

RAINY SEASON by Nicole Phillips

Roads become riverbeds
in Costa Rica

during rainy season.
A local Tico man says:
"People think no one
takes care of the roads.
But it's not true.
Water force is muy fuerte here."
I want to feel the road river
so I walk straight
into the deluge
with a silly little umbrella
in a long white dress.
Yesterday I could balance
on exposed rocks
one by one
to cross the creek.
Today it's a gushing river
the safest way across
is to wade through
the belly of the current
up to my calves.
Shoes wet for days
dress soaked, adobe-red
by splashes
reverberating
from the earth.

Bones

Why are we fascinated by bones? When you think of your
bones, do you see them as a solid, interior structure holding
you up and giving you shape? Or do visualize your bones as

luminescent living tissue, tunneled by marrow where you make your blood? Our language is full of great bone expressions: bone up on something, work your fingers to the bone, I have a bone to pick with you, close to the bone, make no bones about it, and get down to bare bones. We decorate our homes with antlered animal skulls, wave the pirate flag of skull and crossbones across our clothing, display Mexican sugar skulls at Halloween, make an altar to memento mori, remembering we all (have to) die. Many Buddhists meditate with a skull to remind them of the ephemerality of life. Our bones are what's left of this body when we die. How do you feel about death and your mortality? And bones — cool or creepy?

Body/Mindfulness: If you happen to have any bones lying around your home, feel free to get them; otherwise, close your eyes and go inside. Place a hand on a bony protuberance of your body, such as elbow or knee, ankle or wrist, sternum, clavicle, cheekbone, forehead. Give a little tap to your old bones and say hello. Breathe a few tides of in and out while you palpate your bones. Hum into your bones and see if you can feel them buzzing. What do your bones know? Call up any encounters you've ever had with bones.

WRITE NOW! *Tell a bone story. Weave a bone tale. Sing a bone song. Write about your experience with your bones or with someone else's. What comes to mind, and how do you feel when you consider bones? Ever play with a skeleton in anatomy class? Find animal bones in the woods? Debone the fish or meat you plan to eat? How do you feel about bones?*

Examples

BONES by Jo Walker

    sheep skulls
    in long grass fields
    fish skeletons
    on beaches
    bones
    of other species
    brought home
    to mother's chagrin

    i'm a pirating sprite
    on a moonlit night
    collecting bones
    and their dusty moans
    mother's out
    rage
    did not out
    stage
    my satisfaction
    when alone

    I reverently hold
    my bones
    they bring me closer
    to the spirited beyond
    little pieces of death
    reminding me
    that relief
    comes
    soon enough.

BONE SONG by Meredith Heller

Thank you.
For the crystalline minerals
you donated
to fill the holes of sadness
that opened
when I shattered
my right wrist.

I want you to know
that your calcite cathedrals
did not go to waste
but seeded my bones
so I can play guitar
and sing again.

And though my hand will never
be what it once was
a great she-warrior,
I have learned a new way —
the left-hand path,
one that allows me
to hold myself
and others with greater
kindness.

So thank you
for the two small bone ghosts
we grafted onto the branch
of my right radius.

Sure, I wonder who you were.
Did you too play guitar?

Talk with your hands?
Was there someone you loved to touch?

And what part of you now
lives inside me?
Do your circadian rhythms
influence my melodies?

Is that you chanting beside me
as I make bracelets
pushing a prayer
through each tiny bead
my hand steady as steel.

Thank you is the deepest
way I know how to pray
this, and my song.

So I sit with my guitar
fingers picking
across metal strings
singing together
we are greater
than the sum
of our bones.

MEMENTO AMARI, MEMENTO VIVERE by Trisha Coghlan

In Hallstatt, Austria,
a subterranean cave
an ossuary
overlooking an alpine lake
holds more than a thousand skulls

neatly stacked
since the twelfth century
six hundred, delicately hand-painted.

Each deceased soul,
buried fifteen years
in the too-small graveyard,
then rotated
bones stacked underground.

Memento mori,
a reminder to the living
of this life's impermanence.

My heart breaks.
If only I could hold your skull,
softly kiss your eye sockets,
cheekbones, sensitive, brilliant cranium,
try to coax a smile or a poem from you.

I'd delicately paint you
and keep you forever.
It's too late now!
Damn cancer! Damn death!
Damn cremation!
Your entire precious body,
ashes in a box
I can't bear to look at.

This is what we wanted,
for much later,
then, our ashes joining the ocean.
That's some comfort for my anguish.

Another gifted scientist says
molecules of the cremated
return to earth and air
then in new flowers, insects, food,
then birds
and three years later,
many new babies.

I bought a deep-blue orchid.
Our twenty-fifth anniversary.
Gazing at it
hand on my heart,
I see you smile
I write this poem.

CHAPTER 12

Heartbeat

Attune with your heartbeat.

Have you ever heard your own heartbeat? Amazing to know there's this fist-size muscle in your chest pumping blood to your brain and body 24-7. Extraordinary, right? But oh, it is so much more than that. Science now shows what meditators and mystics have always known, that the heart is the true center of our being. The heart is an electromagnetic generator that creates and emits a field of energy. This field attunes and entrains with other electromagnetic fields, like people and animals. Scientists mapping this energetic field found that the heart sends more information to the brain than the brain sends to the heart. The heart has its own nervous system, with about forty thousand neurons, just like the ones in our brains. The heart's electromagnetic field is created by what we feel, and this information is sent to our brains, which helps us to think and act on our feelings. The heart is the captain of the ship, my friends. So how do we live from our hearts? How do we learn to listen, trust, and act on the wise intelligence of our heartland? We can start by tuning in to our actual heartbeat to learn its language, its code, its song.

Listening to Your Heart

Listening and opening communication with your heart is key to living a heart-centered life. Our hearts beat in tune with truth. We can learn to listen to our hearts' unique language. The ear is the new eye; listening is the new seeing. And deep listening is about paying attention with our whole being, wholehearted listening. The most valuable thing we can give to anyone or anything is our attention. Attention is perceived and received as love. Let's practice deep listening, deep loving, with the ear of our hearts from a space of equanimity. Let's learn the language of our hearts.

Body/Mindfulness: Close your beautiful eyes and cozy in. Allow your breath to wash through you in waves. Feel the gentle movement of your chest and belly rise and fall as your breath breathes your body, in and out. Place your hand on your heart — not the spiritual heart in the center of your chest but the actual organ nestled and beating on the left side. With your hand on your heart simply be present with yourself and say hello to this magnificent organ. Now, as if your hand were an ear, listen with your hand until you feel your heartbeat. If you have any problem feeling it, place your fingers on a pulse point at your wrist or neck. You can also lie down on the floor and feel your heart beating either through your back, front, or side body. Experiment to find what works best for you. When you've got a solid connection with your heartbeat, we're going to play a game to open our communication and learn to trust our hearts.

Here we go. Either out loud or within, speak an untruth to yourself, something simple, like a made-up name. For example, I could say, "My name is Samantha Morningstar." Then be aware of how your heart responds under your hand, noticing any shifts in texture, beat, pressure, presence. Just notice. Now tell yourself a corresponding truth, such as your real name, for example, "My name is Meredith Heller." Listen to how your heart responds. Notice any difference in pressure, texture, rhythm. Try another, such as an untruth about where you live, for example, "I live in the jungle." Notice any texture shift from your heart. Now try a corresponding truth, "I live in California." How does your heart respond? People experience a whole range of these shifts in their hearts, such as their heartbeat speeding up or slowing down, a thumping versus a gentle beating, a cessation of beating, a hardening versus a softening of the heart, a feeling of the heart rising to meet your hand when speaking a truth versus your heart sinking and receding from your hand with an untruth. Acknowledge how your heart communicates truth and falsity to you. You are cultivating real-life experiential communication with the deep intelligence and wisdom of your heart organ. Keep practicing to become fluent in the language of your heart. Thank you, heart.

WRITE NOW! *Write about the experience of feeling your heartbeat. What did you notice? What did you learn? How does your heart communicate with you? What differences did you notice in your heartbeat when you told yourself a truth versus an untruth? What does your heart know? Let the words and ideas flow like blood. You're building trust and communication with the wisdom of your heart.*

Examples

MY HEARTBEAT by Korynn Amm

> Tuning in to the rhythm
> my heart beats, thirsty

for the subtle connection, waiting
between the threshold
of fear and vulnerability
depression lies in her bed,
breathing down my back
holding secrets
of doubt and shame.

Tuning in to the rhythm
my breath dives, deep
inside my coiled gut, snaking
its way to find Her, waiting
for me to allow this depth of love.

Tuning in to the rhythm
my hand pressed on my chest, rising up
my breath begins to fill my lungs
my throat aches to be heard
as the ancient tongues of truth
echo the secrets of my soul.

Tuning in to the rhythm
my heart radiates
the sun and moon, bridging
two worlds together,
connecting scars like stars
in this constellation of beauty,
breathing, beating, being
        here now,
                here now.

SOFT HEART by Kathryn Thompson

My heart knows
when I'm here
when I'm not.

When she's hurt
she hardens tightly
a jumbled ball, coarse yarn.

But why so tuff?
Can't she be strong
and also soft?

My heart knows
she can soften
to the fears that arise.

She knows how
to loosen her grip
re-spin herself
smooth as silk.

My heart knows
when I fully show up
I am a beating force of love.
And when I forget
I will place my hand
upon my chest.

And then my heart
says to me
in her own language,

soften — soften
        soften — soften.

Box of Heartbeats

We are heart warriors. Mighty warriors are taught to call up all the most potent experiences of their lives before they go into battle so they are armed with courage and emboldened with true power. We're going to gather all the experiences that make our hearts beat strong and true and put them in a box for later, for when we need to be reminded of what makes our heart beat strong and true. Think time capsule, but heart based.

Body/Mindfulness: Cozy in and close your eyes. Allow your breath to breathe you as you settle in, slow down, arrive. Put your hand on your heart and ask, "Dear heart, what do you beat for, what makes you say yes to life?" Notice what arises for you, which moments, memories, activities, people, places, food, animals, possessions, and experiences make your heart beat. Let these things fill you with your own power.

WRITE NOW! *Write a list of all the things that make your heart beat out a strong, clear yes. Imagine you are filling a box with all things that make your heart happy. If you have trouble choosing, put your hand on your heart and ask. Practice listening. Your heart will always point you in the direction of truth.*

Examples

HEARTBEATS REMEMBERED by Linda B.

> Painted rocks
> Clay-sculpted pioneer girl
> Song of Hiawatha
> Walloping window blind
> Harmonica collection

Autoharp and 175-year-old violin
First pair of drumsticks
First piano lesson book
Letters from Vietnam
State fair postcards from Grandpa
Wildflowers in our woods
Friend Betty's giggle
Silica sand
Hollyhocks & morning glories
Prairies of North Dakota
Ice-cold root beer on hot summer days
Blackjack gum and walnut-crush candy bars
Family reunions
Youth groups and school activities
Yellow roses
Giant pumpkins

MY HEARTBEATS by Jessica Ulrich

My heart beats as a warrior,
she has the strength of a bear
and the kindness of a dog.

My heart beats as a poet,
she writes love songs from within,
whistles happy tunes to fuel her journey.

My heart beats as an artist,
she paints canvases
colorful and bold, calm and patient.

My heart beats as a peacemaker,
she creates equanimity within
teaching my body to relax.

My heart beats as a lover,
she shares her stories and her secrets
appreciating the simple things.

Holy Heartbreak

We've all experienced heartbreak. I don't think any of us get
out of here without it. I think it's hardwired, or heartwired,
into the human experience. Heartbreak comes in many forms:
relationships or friendships ending; illness, injury, death of
loved ones; loss or change of home, employment, or mental
or physical capacity. Come with me now into the land of holy
heartbreak. Heartbreak can be a doorway. Instead of bypass-
ing our pain, let's acknowledge it, voice it, and harvest the
understanding of how, rather than being an obstacle on our
path, pain *is* our path. If we're lucky, heartbreak arrives and
dismembers everything we know, presenting us with a growth
node, to deepen and be more present, accepting, compassionate, sovereign, and heart centered.

Body/Mindfulness: Close your beautiful eyes and go inside.
Ride the waves of your breath in and out, as your body and
heart soften and open. Place your hand on your heart or pulse
point and attune with your heartbeat. Ask your heart which
heartbreak, current or past, is ready for your deep listening,
attention, love. When you know which one you want to work
with, recall what happened. Notice all the sensations and feelings that arise for you with this heartbreak. Don't push them
away; invite them in. Allow yourself to feel all the feels, the
hurt, pain, and loss. Keep breathing. Keep loving yourself.
Stay with it until you feel something shift, until you soften
into tenderness with yourself, and perhaps until your tears
come to cleanse you.

WRITE NOW! *Start by naming the heartbreak. What caused your heart to hurt and break? Next, give voice to what hurts, the loss, sorrow, depression, betrayal, abandonment, anger, illness, injury, loneliness. Give yourself space to listen to and voice all your feelings associated with this event. Give yourself your full attention, bringing your compassionate curiosity. Then write to discover how this heartbreak serves as your path to breaking open. When and how did it change from heartbreak to heart open? Finally, what is the growth node or opportunity of this heartbreak? How has this holy heartbreak helped you to break holy open? How has it changed you, the way you live, your relationship with yourself and others?*

Examples

PERFECT BOY by Diana Rush

> He wasn't the child I dreamed of,
> but I don't think I was the mother he dreamed of either.
> When he came to us as a baby,
> the first words he heard me say were "I love you."
> I meant them then, and now I mean them even more.
>
> The months passing by told us there was something
> different
> about our boy, but it was hard to name.
> He reached for a bee, got stung, cried, then reached for
> another.
> He spoke words, beautiful words. Then they disappeared.
> He didn't grow, didn't slow down, didn't understand.
>
> I was wrong when I thought time would "fix" him.
> Medicine would "fix" him.
> The right school would "fix" him.

What became fixed was my tendency to see only what he
    couldn't do.

A new friend of mine met him and stared at him in
    wonder.
She watched as he hugged everyone in the room.
She listened as he talked about the green garbage truck
that drove by on Wednesdays.
She heard as he sang to the music on the radio.
In awe she said to me,
"He is the most perfect human I have ever met."
My sweet boy.
Perfect.

I looked at him so I could see him the way she did.
What he couldn't do paled in comparison to what he
    could.
He didn't need to be fixed.
My heart did and my head did.
And it was.

BEWARE THE CATBIRD by Jac-Lynn Stark

Your well-practiced mating dance lured me in
my heart unguarded
love poured out
like an unstoppable fountain
our bodies so in tune
yet our voices clashed
jarring and discordant.
Like you, the catbird has many voices.
It can sound like a robin
a tree frog

a hawk on the wing
the more voices he has
the more mates he can choose from
but which voice is his own?
You used your voices to speak in riddles
pretending ambiguity was a form of kindness.

The catbird wears a plain gray cap every day
yet you are the man with many hats
always a new persona to draw attention
posting daily affirmations to attract likes
yet you hardly ever follow them.
I tried not to see your empty soul
disguised behind colorful plumage.
The catbird flicks his tail and flashes
his chestnut belly to attract a mate
but has another in a nest nearby
like you, always another woman waiting
all of us replaceable objects
to feed your hungry ego.

Our almost relationship never got off the ground
an injured bird that could not fly
you'd fight against any perceived restriction
fly elsewhere with any whim or gust of wind
you flew away from me and my heart felt numb
the darkening days reflecting my inner sorrow.

But now time has passed
and I feel good to fly solo
knowing more about what to watch for
the next time someone's feathers catch my eye.

Heart Ally

We have been gathering a council of spirit animals to call on when we need guidance. Today we will meet the special animal that is ally and companion to your heart. From a liminal, nonthinking mind space, you will journey to meet your heart's ally, the one who has come to help you listen and stay true to your heart. Allow a new animal to choose you for this journey, one you have not worked with before. Perhaps they offer their wild nature, their strength, wisdom, skill, clarity, trust, intuition, instinct, savvy, ferocity, tenderness, sensuality, truth, cooperation, pack mind, discernment, survival. What else? Let's find out!

Body/Mindfulness: Close your eyes and arrive inside. Breathe yourself into a deep and open state. Go to your favorite place in nature or your inner sanctuary to meet your heart ally. Clear your mind and allow an animal to come forward and choose you, one who offers their unique genius to help you live in deeper communion with your heart. Be open and curious. Which animal is here to be companion to your heart? Trust the one who shows up. When one chooses you, welcome them into your heart. Breathe and be present with this animal. What an honor! Explore what it feels like to have this animal as your heart's ally. Why did they choose you? What is it about this animal that helps you be true to your heart?

WRITE NOW! *Write about your experience with your heart ally. What does it feel like to have this animal as your heart's companion? What does this animal offer you in terms of its wild, instinctual knowing? How did you know this was your heart animal? How did it choose you? How do you apply this animal's unique genius to inform your life and heart?*

Examples

GRANDMOTHER WHALE by Verana Bailowitz

> Grandmother Whale,
> birthed from the Great Thaw,
> you are slow and colossal
> you hold all ancient memory,
> you are the soul of the earth.
> The Great Songstress
> of the original Song,
> you click and smack
> with melody and rhythm.
>
> My grandmother
> who recently passed over
> swam out to meet you,
> heard your melodies
> and followed you
> out to sea.
>
> Now you sing the songs together
> angels of the deep blue.
> You weave horror and mystery
> threaded through melodies
> of compassion.
> You call all souls home.
>
> Old Grandmother Whale,
> a timeless bubble escapes
> from your single sacred hole.
> Each of your breaths, a miracle,
> a holy reminder
> of life's primordial gurgle

announcing … I live. I live.
I slow my heartbeat
to full cosmic thuds.
I guide and glide my blood
with smooth, blue tides.
I open my wide water wings
carrying my grandmother
on my smooth, shiny back.

I am a whale wearing pearls,
floating, knowing, drifting
in currents of ancient grace.

My grandmother is lost at sea
dead now and finding her way.
We are carrying her.
We are singing her home.

BEE INCANTATION by Jac-Lynn Stark

Enter my heart, bees
let me feel you buzz inside me
exploring the nooks and crannies
of this muscle that works so hard
its stored hurts, joys, dormant emotions.

Fly from chamber to chamber
looking for places that need to wake
from soporific slumber
let this buzzing vibrate my body
wake up the numb places
with a tickling caress
a kind of internal bee massage
to loosen up what's buried.

Give me your heightened ability to find what I need
your fearless venturing into unknown territories
flying from one group of blossoms to another
no sitting on top of a dead flower until you die of
    starvation
when blooms await you in every direction
with their holy nectar.

Help me find an inner compass to guide me
leave behind the waffling back and forth
on the knife edge of indecision and doubt
even though both sides of this sharp edge
where I perch in tortured inertia
have gifts to offer me.

Teach me how to store up what delights my heart
the shapes of clouds, the sounds of birds,
the moon, always the moon.
You gather pollen and store it on your body
to bring home so you will have enough
when no flowers can be found.

Help me store my own delights
so when I feel despair
I don't get caught in that black vortex
that always waits to suck me in
twirl me around in a tornado of darkness and debris
that feels like I will never emerge.

Help me feel like I am part of a tribe
and that I have something to share.
Like you help your sisters find pollen
by dancing a special dance

let my words be pathways
I share to help others.

Yesterday I felt you inside me in yoga class
buzzing happily, an internal *om*
it felt like there were two of you.
Invite your sisters to stay with me
through this winter,
making honey inside my heart.

Heart Vow

What would your life and relationships look and feel like if you lived deeply devoted to your heart? What are the essential elements of your commitment to yourself? What vows can you make to your heart that allow you to be fully you, to shine big, to go fallow, to make mistakes, to be fully seen and loved, to change and grow, to say yes when you mean yes, and no when you mean no, to live with sovereignty in your own heartland, as if you were the queen of your own heart? Because guess what? You are!

Body/Mindfulness: Close your eyes and go inside. Get comfy. Surf the waves of your breath in and out. Allow your body to soften. Breathe right into the center of your heart, through all the layers of pain, loss, and separation until you breathe yourself back into belonging. Place your hand on your heart and listen for the message you most need to hear right now to feel safe, held, and loved. Perhaps that message is: I believe in you, or you've got this, or you're going to be OK, or you are loved, or I'm here with you, or I've got you. Trust your heart.

WRITE NOW! *Write your heart vows. Write as many as you wish until you touch every vow you've ever needed to hear. Then vow to yourself to be fully committed to your heart. This might sound like: I am devoted to your peace, truth, and joy. I promise to hold and protect you. I promise to listen to your knowing, your wisdom, your needs, your desires. I belong to you, and you belong to me. I pledge allegiance to my heart.*

Examples

DEAR HEART by Kimberly Gallagher

Oh, dear heart, I am thankful
for your strong, constant beating
within my chest.

For the clarity and wisdom
you offer
with each strong beat.

Today, love, I vow to listen
and listen deeply
whenever I am questioning.

I vow to trust
your heartbeat messages
and to act accordingly.

I vow to stay true to my inner knowing
despite the shouting, shaming voices
that clamor for my attention.

I vow to make time
to feel my magic
and to practice wielding it.

I am a powerful, wild she-witch
a force of nature
a force *for* nature.

Your drumbeat
heartbeat
always my guide.

DEVOTED by Tiana Cicco

How do I channel a volcano?
How do I swallow the stars?
How do I paint the worlds between dreaming and
    waking?

How do I cry a million dewdrops without melting?
How do I defy gravity's tug and just drift with the
    clouds?
How do I wrestle a bear from her warm cave and open
    her sleepy eyes to daylight?

How do I reassemble the shards of a mirror without
    tearing my pride?
How do I teach a wild serpent to bite only evil hands?
How do I smile at disaster without cutting my teeth?

How do I forgive a giant meteor careening toward earth?
How do I resonate with the echoes of tomorrow's grief?
How do I trust my instinct when no one else believes me?

How do I expose the chambers of my heart without
    becoming filleted?
How do I bottle a lightning bolt and press it into
    medicine?
How do I save society with only a wink and a handful of
    wildflowers?

How? I must become a magician.
To be truly devoted to myself
this is what I must do.

CHAPTER 13

Moon Dance

Follow the lunar phases to inhabit your cycles,
your shadow, your shine.

Women have an innate and intimate connection with the moon. We are both, by nature, cyclical. We look to Grandmother Moon, who has been dancing the cycles of light and dark for eons, and ask for her wise counsel to help us navigate our own cycles that make us whole. Moon pulls the tides of our water and blood as she turns through her phases, as women do in their menstrual cycles. Moon is often associated with moods. Moody moon, moody women. You know how some people get jazzed up during a full moon? We used to refer to people highly influenced by the phases of the moon as lunatics, meaning moon-sick. I just learned that in Italian you don't say a woman is in a bad mood, you say *her moon is crooked.* I love that!

Moon represents powerful feminine energy: intuition, deep psyche, wisdom, passion, sexuality, hormones, cycles of birth and death, light and dark. Moon mirrors the depth of our wholeness as women. Each lunar phase offers a slightly different opportunity of focus. New moon is a birthing time for new ideas and energy. As the moon waxes, we build and cultivate what we've birthed. Full moon is a time of culmination and harvesting that which we put into motion on the new moon. During the waning moon, we wind down, emptying ourselves before we begin again. Moon cycle is akin to seed cycle: a seed sprouts, buds, flowers, turns back to seed, dies, releases, and repeats. Attuning to moon energy helps us embrace this natural rhythm of life as we tend to the birth, growth, release, and renewal of our ideas, projects, and dreams.

In this chapter we'll practice cultivating communication with our deep psyche, which the moon represents. Moon language and moon metaphor come from the deepest part of our beings. We want to touch that part and write from there. What we find won't always make logical sense, but stay with it, and moon will teach us her rhythms. Let's write along with the dance of the moon cycles as we learn to inhabit our shadow and our shine.

Dance of the Moon Cycles

> **New moon:** birthing/setting intentions
> **First quarter:** gathering/tending
> **Full moon:** harvest/celebration
> **Last quarter:** letting go/gratitude

New Moon

New moon is a time to refresh, recharge, and resource. We are coming out of the dark and beginning again. The light is birthing, budding. It's an opportunity to set new intentions, planting new seeds and new dreams. What you put your attention on grows. Let's get clear about what new seed dreams you're planting and where you're putting your attention this new moon.

New Moon Seeds: Quick Write (Five Minutes)

Light a candle and breathe with the flame. Allow it to warm you, help you focus, and spark your ideas. Write ten to twenty new moon seeds, that is, what you're putting your attention and intention on this new moon cycle.

Examples of New Moon Seeds

> Simplifying my home
> Making nourishing food
> Taking baths
> Making music with friends
> Writing a gratitude list
> Saying no to excess sugar
> Practicing positive self-talk
> Looking for a new job
> Going for daily walks
> Taking an art class
> Making time to rest

Body/Mindfulness: Grab your eye mask or scarf and place it over your eyes. Close your eyes and cozy in. Feel the support of what's underneath and behind you. Invite your body to feel held as you soften, melt open, and arrive inside. Allow your breath to find you. With your eye mask covering your eyes to block out the light, allow yourself to absorb the darkness. Relax and let go into this darkness. Drink it in like an elixir. Pure presence. Place your hands on your moon belly and listen in. Is she empty or full? Is she calm or agitated? What does she need to feel nourished and fed, satiated, soft, and open? This *listening in* is a holistic practice. As we attune and attend to our needs, we teach ourselves to be present and meet what's up for us, in each new moment, each new phase. This listening in is the attention we cultivate when we write. Listen in to your belly, to this moment, and notice what's bubbling up for you right now. What calls your attention? What new seeds do you want to plant on this new moon?

WRITE NOW! *Write about what you felt bubbling up when you listened in to your moon belly. What new ideas, projects, seeds, and dreams will you focus on this new moon cycle?*

Examples

MOONSEEDS by Robyn Morgan

> I'm going to plant some moonseeds
> in my night garden
> water them with my sweat.
> I'm going to work this soil until it sings
> I'm going to make offerings
> of fire and bone
> and shadow from my dark side.
> I'm going to turn these tears
> to trumpet vines
> then climb them
> to the roof of this old house
> where I will sit
> and point
> at the stars.

MOON LADDER by Mary Pritchard

> The moon envelops me
> in her dark gossamer
> her light waning.

Like her I have plummeted
to my darkest depth
with no hope in my heart.

Moon offered me a ladder
to clamber up and see her
budding with new life.

She offered me gifts
found only in darkness
pulled all the way down
into pain and anguish.

There is beauty in the deep
surrendering to emptiness
sitting silently in the heart
of the moon's darkness.

Here I await my tender rebirth
when I will feel her soft stroke
of renewal.

New moon, new life
wholeness
from the dark.

Waxing Crescent — First Quarter

The light is growing. We are building, gathering, tending our seeds. We are watering and sunning our dreams with our attention. There is a sense of excitement for the journey ahead. We are becoming. We are moonifesting!

One of the things we need to tend as we grow older is keeping our imaginations alive. Imagination is one of the deepest, most intimate, and powerful aspects of consciousness. When we engage our imaginations, we are in a state of deep play in which we are open, un-self-conscious, and in the flow. We say yes to what arises, we experiment and explore, collaborating with our creativity. Today we draw on our imaginations to write a recipe for a moon elixir. An elixir is a potion that makes us strong and vital, gives us the courage to be true to ourselves, to realize and live our passion and purpose. We will gather the ingredients for our elixir as the moon gathers her light.

Body/Mindfulness: Cozy in and close your moon eyes. Allow your breath to breathe you in waves. Feel supported by whatever is underneath or behind you, as your body softens and melts open. Arrive in your inner moonscape, where everything is possible. Imagine you are traveling through the cosmos and gathering all the ingredients you need to make a moon elixir to heal and energize your life force. You may collect both practical and magical ingredients. For example, you may add a dollop of bone broth and an explosion of stars. You may add a bead of wildflower honey along with an exhale of dinosaur breath. Go harvest what you need.

WRITE NOW! *Write about all the ingredients you gathered for your moon elixir. Follow the recipe below, including ingredients, process, and how to serve, just like when you're cooking something delicious.*

Recipe for a Moon Elixir

1. Ingredients
2. Process
3. How to serve

Examples

MOON ELIXIR FOR THE PASSIONATE HEART
by Tanya Flanagin

Ingredients:
A soft self-hug filled with warm reverence
A solitary swim with the gray whales by a magic island
A single, silly romp through a garden wet with rain
3 howls at the moon, ow, ow, owwwwooo
1 cup of crow watching
A dash of sunset
2 teaspoons of rose-scented whispers
1 passionate tango dance beneath a sparkling night sky
A fortnight of circle gathering with sisters of the goddess
2 cups of risk, spiked with courage
Followed by a wild night of lovemaking
A pinch, just a pinch of sunrise

Instructions:
Carefully combine ingredients in the purplest of glass
    bottles and place beneath the new moon for thirteen
    and a half days.

How to Serve:
For best results get naked and dance ferociously with
    friends beneath a full moon and howl more, ow, ow,
    owwwwooo.

MOON ELIXIR by Mireya Quirie

One prayer. Whispered. Then shouted. Over a cliff. Start
with "Helllooooo???"

Even if there's no echo, draw out the *oooo* sound.

(Just one per elixir. Two can be overpowering.)

One spit. That's for chutzpah.

One deep inhale of my lover's armpit.

As many rainbow bubbles as shake out from my smooth
madrone barrels.

A spoonful of last night's nourishing leftovers that
contain leafy greens, locally grown.

A generous splash of the worst coffee I've ever had from
a gas station while waiting for my brake pads to be
changed by a cutie with grease-stained jeans on a
rural highway far from home.

A double shot of that sudden spring ceanothus scent that
slams me as I walk outside.

One of my tia's tortillas filled with a generous helping of
my tio's arroz con pollo.

A long hug from someone who adores me.

A loud cheek smooch from my sweetie.

One tablespoon of mud scrapings from my last hike.

A smack on my ass from the one who motivates me to
keep on keepin' on.

One teardrop shed in the canned peaches aisle that
surprised me with its heartache.

Two dropperfuls of puddle water in the sand at my feet
after a midnight full moon ocean dive.

Pour equally into the four cobalt-blue glass goblets I
collected from a free box on Haight Street.

Splash on a mid-priced tequila reposado and light with
a strike-anywhere match, preferably one found in a
jacket pocket from last week's campfire.

Share with three carefully chosen others, keeping one for
myself.
Now drink deeply while murmuring this chant:
"I have experienced so much.
I hold my soul, as I hold yours,
with tenderness and love and laughter
for all that has been and all that will be."

Full Moon

On the full moon our emotions, creativity, and intuition peak.
We may feel energized, drained, or even slightly manic. The
key is to stay present with full moon energy, learning to ride
the currents wherever they go, up, down, in, out. Stay the
course and take stock of how the seeds you planted on the
new moon have bloomed. Be open to reap and receive the harvest of your good work. Full moon is a time of culmination,
reward, celebration. Share this time with others who support
your projects and dreams.

To celebrate the full moon, we're going to write a moon
personification. *Personification* means giving human qualities
to something nonhuman. In other words, we're going to turn
the moon into a person or magical being. Ready?!

Body/Mindfulness: Cozy in and arrive, taking a seat within
your inner being. Breathe yourself into a state of deep receptivity. When you feel yourself soften and open, imagine the
full moon as if it were a wise and magical being. Engage your
imagination and allow this magical moon-being to approach
you. How do they look? What is their energy? How do they
move and communicate? How do you feel in their presence?
Do they have a gift or message for you?

WRITE NOW! *Write about your encounter with this magical moon-being. Use the questions below to help you imagine and describe them.*

Questions for Your Magical Moon-Being

- Where were they born?
- How old are they?
- What do they look like?
- What are they wearing?
- How do they move?
- How do they communicate with you?
- What are their favorite things?
- Who are their friends?
- What are their fears and dreams?
- What is their favorite food?
- What makes them happy or sad?
- What are their strengths and weaknesses?
- Do they play an instrument or a sport, practice an art form?
- What inspires them? What is their mission?
- What gift, message, or wisdom do they have for you?
- How do you feel in their presence?

Examples

QUEEN OF SILVER GLOW by Ann McGuire

> A gossamer orb
> rides down a moonbeam
> straight to my heart
> petals open
> to reveal a Queen

of Silver Glow.
She radiates gentleness
speaks in harmonies
of gold and platinum.
She is dressed in beauty,
sheaves of delicate clouds
swirl a gown
detailed in diamonds.
She is crowned
with the stars of Virgo
and carries her power quietly,
revealing it only in the promise
of her smile.
She looks clearly into my eyes
and says, "All you want,
all you desire,
has always been
within you."
She lifts her wand
like an artist lifts their brush,
and paints me with light.

MOON BEAR by Verana Bailowitz

We lock eyes
from across the starlit dance floor
she sways her wide hips
and saunters, lumbering my way.
A sigh shudders through me
as wild anticipation leads,
as quiet trusting heart follows
as the quiet trusting heart leads
as the radiant unknown follows.

She comes closer
her presence pulses
like a thick white aorta,
feeding my eyes,
filling my veins,
I take her in
Great Mother Lungs
I long to be held by her.

Even closer now
I can hear her raw breath
gruff, I am surprised,
like a great bear
she breathes
with the whole earth
keeping the beat
in the great domed den,
as I begin to soften
and rest under her protective gaze
I am folded into her broad ribs
as everything else turns
to witness our dance,

Her strong, open arms lead our way
knowing and padded
the path is clearly painted
across the ecliptic trim of my skirt
I am twirled and whirled
she spirals me deep
I need nothing
not even water to be alive like this.

Moon Bear
I am home in your immensity
all of me
longing
belonging
to you
to myself
in your great glorious presence
holding me as I learn to hold me.

Waning Crescent — Last Quarter

The waning moon signifies completion. This is a time of letting go with gratitude for all you have received and achieved during the full moon harvest. Your metaphorical crops are in abundance. You've reaped the fruition of your intentions and projects. You may feel generous and want to share your fortune with others. After the celebration, in your own rhythm, begin to release and let go. Like the moon gradually letting go of her size and her light, you can let go of this cycle and, with it, anything you no longer need.

Examples

WANING WOLF MOON by Jeannie McKenzie

We felt your glorious howling
wolf presence
calling the clans together
the lost souls
the dark parts
that flush with anger and frustration
the unseen parts.

You bathe them in your brilliance
let them glow in the spotlight
all our conflicting wounds
laid out on the mountaintop before you
howling their piece of the truth.

You shoulder the burden of our deepest grief
unravel the layers
night by night
in your infinite arms of compassion
carry it all back
into the fertile womb of darkness.

Slowly interlace
in the mirror of opposites
until all that is left
is the empty night
reminding us
that we too have the capacity to hold
this infinite darkness
in our arms.

HOLY PURPLE GARDENERS by Verana Bailowitz

Tiny dark-lilac moon
peeking out behind
rusty billowing clouds
dark-purple bloom
I almost missed you
almost rushed by on my way
seeking presence
in all the wrong places.

Yet here you are, always
breathing quietly in the night
planted from the deepest seed of time
your stem breaks through my center
roots wide and remembering
your leaves lift
and wrap around my breasts
honoring, blessing my changing body.

The tiny hairs on your lavender leaves
brushing my own star-kissed skin
have I forgotten how active babies are at night?
How when the moon rises,
the wise ones lift and whisper stories
of old men falling in love
of hearts thawing in warm, emerald pools
of wildcats stretching and sleeping and dreaming
    together
of a world made whole by time itself.

Lilac dream,
your thousand petals pour out of my eyes
I turn belly down
my womb pushing petals
each seed deeper into the earth
watering each one with my tears
of love and grief and care
for a world that's gone mad and forgotten
that the most exquisite flowers
are planted in the dark,
the most potent dreams are tended
by the holy purple gardeners

who water each of us
tending and waiting patiently
to weave wise whispers
in our innocent, infant fears
and tuck us in and ready us
for the golden tomorrow.

Dark Moon

Before the new moon, we sit with the dark moon. This is an in-between time, like the pause between inhale and exhale. Come join me here in the dreaming, the fertile darkness, the unknown, the death that precedes the new beginning. This is the secret place, the shadow space, where we surrender who we are and what we think we know. Where we learn to wait until the new is ready to raise its wild head from the dark soil of being. This moon phase is often overlooked in our culture; we are always on, in a hurry, measuring ourselves by our accomplishments, our doings. Everything in nature, including us, has a fallow period. We forget that unplugging is as necessary to the fruition of any dream or garden as is the labor. Rest is essential; it repairs and recycles. It renews us. We must empty to make room for the new. We must be willing to give ourselves back to pure beingness, weightless and free-floating. Back to the great unknown and undoing before new ideas can dream themselves through us. Welcome to the dark moon.

Body/Mindfulness: Grab your eye mask. Cozy in and close your eyes. Feel supported by what's underneath and behind you. Give yourself to gravity. Allow your breath to find and breathe you into deep beingness, intimacy with your dark inner moon. Feel yourself being held here in this holy darkness. Nothing to do. Nowhere to go. No one to become. Just floating here in beingness, both empty and full. Breathe it all the way into the stardust of your bones. From this place of shimmering darkness, say hello to yourself and know the dark as part of your wholeness. What medicine lives here on the dark side of your moon? Sense into anything you're ready to surrender, dissolve, forgive, return to the great darkness to be recycled and renewed.

WRITE NOW! *Write about your experience with the dark moon. How did you feel there in the dark? What did you sense? Could you let go and let yourself be nourished in the nothingness? What did you feel ready to surrender, forgive, return to the great darkness?*

Examples

HONORING THE EMPTY MOON by Jeannie McKenzie

> The last part of the exhalation
> the last gasping of tears
> the final letting go
> scraping out the last bits
> squeezing out every last morsel
> before the new rushes in.
> Howling wind whisks
> the last of the old leaves
> the bits that thought to hang on
> rallied and railed in resistance
> resign now to release.
>
> Terse and tired
> this fallow phase of emptying

this slack tide of my spirit
begs for nothing
no new ideas
no new impulses
no seeds to sow
less is more now.

Lie fallow
let boredom be its own compost
aimless, the bow is not yet drawn back
not even a pondering of prey
in my life of doing
honoring the empty
is an exercise I fail at regularly
reigniting my imagination
with false stimulants
of internet and chocolate
pushing for more
and now I push for more... emptiness?
No!

I will sit with a tree
let my sap flow down
simply surrender to gravity
as it overtakes this moment
wraps me in the quiet heartbeat
of the resting earth
where we are all held
in the dark arms
of moon.

CLEAN BURN by Bianca Amira Zanella

Engulf me;
      fire —
let tonight take hold.
I am your kindling —
a worn pine bough
dry with tradition
no tinsel, it's safe
to burn, I promise.
I, broken, promise
I'll go up quickly.

If I am to let go
of the stories
that slow this sap of self —
fire, you'll hardly remember
how much space I tried to fill.

In an instant, I am yours.
Fully and finitely, only then —
I belong to smoke like sage,
cleansing shall be my legacy.
I will leave no ash, no char behind.

I give branch by branch, working
like doves. Needle stitches like my
seamstress grandmother on her
wedding night, until all that lingers on
the wind is a thread of dishonest days.

CHAPTER 14

Metamorphosis

Embody the poetry of change.

Life is change. Change makes us healthy and resilient. But it can also make us crazy! It calls on us to shift and adapt. It needs us to let go of who and what we are to become something new. The more we can embrace change, the better we can flow with life. In this chapter we will practice conscious change, honing our capacity to embody and dance with the poetry of change.

Using butterfly metamorphosis as our map, we will write our way through the process of change by exploring each stage from egg to caterpillar, chrysalis to emerging adult, and finally, butterfly. You can't force or hurry your way through change. You can't pull the petals of a flower open and expect it to survive or crack a bird from its shell and expect it to have the strength to fly. Each stage is necessary. Give yourself the time and space to fully explore and inhabit each phase of this process without pushing into the next until you are good and ready.

Think about what kind of changes you are experiencing in your life right now. Perhaps you are in a cycle of change with your work, home, relationship, health, sexuality, lifestyle, purpose, creativity, or community. Whatever you're working with, I invite you to have an open mind, to be willing not to know what or who you may become, and to trust that change is natural and necessary. Allow your writing to be a journey of discovery. Trust the process to change you into an ever-deeper, stronger, more fully alive *you*!

Egg

We'll begin at the very beginning, in the egg, contained safely in a shell, in the dark. Egg is sacred, depicted across all cultures and all mystery schools as the symbol of life. *Egg* and *seed* are synonymous. Both eggs and seeds contain all the nutrients and knowledge needed for growing into an adult. We all know the great Zen koan "Which came first, the chicken or the egg?" The beauty with koans is that you can't think yourself into or out of them. You can only sit with them and allow them to be. So too with the egg and the process of change. Let's sit with the mystery as we explore the egg stage.

Body/Mindfulness: Put on your eye mask, cozy in, and arrive in yourself. Find your breath and allow it to fill and empty you, easefully. Imagine either that you are inside an egg or that you are an egg, whichever works best for you. Allow yourself to be held inside the dark safety and protection of your egg before you need to become or do anything. How does it feel to be held in this holy darkness in the space before becoming? Imagine your sacred shell. You know yourself by feel. You float within the smooth calcite capsule of your egg world. Perhaps you rock side to side with your heartbeat, testing the boundaries, stretching edge to edge, leaning into safety. You do not need to know who or what you'll become. Simply nuzzle into the darkness of your egg, where you are held. You are complete. You are whole. You are egging.

WRITE NOW! *Write about your experience in or as the egg. What does it feel like to egg? What did you learn about yourself as egg?*

Examples

JOURNEY OF TRUST by Lisa Eddy

> I am safe and protected
> as an egg
>
> I feel a level of contentment
> a trust of being,
> never before experienced
>
> I have a sense of knowing the value
> of this dark fertile time of stillness
>
> I understand this total embracing
> is an essential part of my journey
>
> For the first time
> I'm not reaching outside myself
> to find answers
>
> I understand I am the source
> of light in this darkness
>
> I am the spark of hope
> I am the rich unknown
> I am never alone
>
> While I trust source
> I realize I am source

In the darkness
I have found my light
my faith
my true beauty.

WITHIN THE EGG by Rhiannon Lynn

The smooth darkness envelops me in a safety that is
unfamiliar in my waking walk. A sense of acceptance for
all things. A simple knowing that the complexity of the
ever-present symphony of all that's within and all that's
without dances with purpose.

There is a softness to this darkness. A gentle release of
all tensions that long to make meaning with every note
of music that is happening. That pathologizing voice
quieted, letting the heartbeat of knowing lead the gentle
trusting.

A boundary of immunity, a sense of security, an easeful
harmony with all that exists in this present moment's
gracious gifting. A new awareness of receptivity that
is not disrupted by that which is engaging, rather a
witnessing, a nod of acknowledgment that causes no
distraction from the safety of my egg environment.

A breathing womb of quiet buffers the intensity of all
that is not me. Allowing the sounds and sensations
to carry on with their autonomous navigations while
I lovingly sway inside my egg. How liberating not to
be pulled in any direction, to have my nervous system
maintain its sense of being held and nurtured.

All the while, life continues to be inside and outside me. A newfound clarity: all that's occurring is not my responsibility. I am not required to adapt tirelessly to the needs of those around me.

I am a being of sovereignty, and this egg, my space of safety, is a birthright I carry. I can witness and be, without expectation, without a contract of identity that is externally projected on me. I can just be, fortified in my boundaries, resourced in my safety, nourished as a baby.

Caterpillar

Metamorphosis is all about shapeshifting. We are born shape-shifters. Think about how your body has changed since you were a child. Society conditions us to stay the same, to hold one shape and one identity our whole lives in order to be safe, but the truth is that safety lies in changing and adapting. Our capacity to survive and thrive is directly proportional to our capacity to change. Today we will break out of the safe container of our egg and shapeshift into our new form, caterpillar! How do we do this? How do we break out of the egg? What tool or resource do we use? Let's find out.

Body/Mindfulness: Cozy in and arrive. Allow your breath to find you and open you. Now imagine yourself back in your egg. Take one last deep breath of your life as an egg. Anchor this feeling so you can return whenever you need. But you have outgrown your shell, and now it is only a barrier preventing you from nourishing yourself as you grow and change.

What do you need to whisper into your own ear to call up your strength and crack yourself out of the egg? Clear your mind, and open your nondominant hand, allowing a tool to appear. It can be anything. It doesn't need to be logical or literal. We are in the realm of imagination. Trust your deep psyche. Say yes to whatever appears. Pick up your tool, whether a solid object or a feeling, and start chipping away at the shell that once did its good work to protect you. Come on out now, caterpillar, it's time to feast!

WRITE NOW!   *Write about what tool showed up in your hand. What meaning does it have for you? How did you use it to crack your way out?*

Examples

FREEDOM by Liz Laurel

> As I sit in darkness
> my cozy space
> between worlds
> now too constraining
> I must find my way out.
> I search what little room exists in here
> and where there was once only me
> something new appears —
> a long feather, glimmering
> blue and green and purple-eyed on one end
> hard and strong and sharp-quilled on the other.
> I pick it up, feeling its lightness
> I caress my body with its softness
> it dances across every inch of me,

lighting up my senses.
Suddenly I feel a sting
the sharp end pricks my finger
my blood pools in a dot.
Dipping the quill
into my blood ink
I write:
  FREEDOM
emblazoning the inside of the eggshell wall
that once encapsulated me, protecting me
from the world outside.
This lights a fire inside me to escape
and not knowing what to do with all this big energy
I grasp my feather tightly and pull my arm back.
With the weight of my entire being behind me
I take the hard, strong, sharp end of my feather
and punch through these confining walls
bursting into the bright expansive world beyond.

HEART FIRST by Kimberly Gallagher

It was the shining
of the full round moon
against the blue sky
this morning
and the glorious
unapologetic beauty
of the red amaryllis
blossoming in my sunroom
its six yellow stamens
waving from its center
that coaxed me out
of my inward curl.

I felt my heart
reaching toward
this breathtaking beauty
my arms and legs
stretching, pushing
harder against familiar edges
my whole body swelling
with the need
to move beyond them.

I felt the pen in my left hand
the thick, flowered one
I took from my mom's desk
after she died.

This pen
tool of my voice
my confidence
my will.

With it I draw a door
of shimmering moonlight.

It swings open
revealing the full glory
of that voluptuous
red amaryllis,
that shining
white moon
against the blue.

I tumble out
heart first

into the wild beauty
of the waiting world.

Chrysalis

This is the deepest stage of metamorphosis where we will completely let go of our form and turn into *goo*! The hard shell of our chrysalis will protect us as we break down old energy patterns and reinvent ourselves with wings. What do you need to let go, undo, unstructure, unlearn, or unbecome to imagine yourself anew? What patterns, habits, or ways of being no longer serve you, hold you down, hold you back from being fully winged and ready to fly? Let's acknowledge what no longer serves us and give it up to the great goo, or as my students like to say, the great goo-roo who transforms old energy into something new, something better, something of our choosing!

Quick Write (Five Minutes)

Write a list of five to ten things that no longer serve you and that you're ready to give over to the great goo.

Examples of What to Give to the Great Goo

Keeping myself small
Minimizing or ignoring my needs
Procrastinating or freezing
Doubting my competence
Questioning my purpose
Judgment
Anxiety
Depression

Isolation
Competition
Addiction

Body/Mindfulness: Cozy in and arrive. Imagine you have a big bubbling pot of goo on the stove. Name each thing you're giving to the goo to be melted. Allow old patterns and old ways of being to dissolve into the goo. Enjoy the goo. When you're ready, put yourself into the goo to be melted. Sit for a moment in the goo, where you're completely dissolved and where you haven't yet formed into anything new and all possibilities await you. Now, not from thinking your way there but from allowing deep psyche, your muse, angels, or guides to show you (in whatever way they do), two new necessary ways of being, like the nubs of two shiny new wings that will grow and support you, lifting you into this next phase of life.

WRITE NOW! *Write about your experience with giving it all to the great goo to be melted. What did you give to the goo? Then write about the two new wing buds or ways of being that are emerging to serve you on your journey of aliveness, becoming fully you!*

Examples

GIVE IT TO THE GOO by Kathryn Thompson

> The smell of burning flesh takes me over
> as I shove my everlasting need to fix myself
> into the glistening goo.
> The taste of fear permeates my mouth:

What will I be?
Who will I be?
Without this empty brokenness.

My trembling hands pick up the shovel
heaving in decades of not wanting to be here
not wanting to be alive
a wealth of eating disorders
comparing and manipulating my body
to morph to their unrealistic idea of beauty.

There is one last heap of debris
perhaps the messiest of them all
the victim card —
I thank the card for protecting me
and shaping me so tenderly
then I kick its dusty remains into the goo
I don't need you anymore!

The goo takes it all and digests it
into spring nettle soup
I slurp it down
feeling the vitality it provides
so nourishing that I begin to feel
two tiny feathers tickle my back.

The sun beams through the clouds
morning birds flutter down bearing messages
in their beaks, gold satin ribbons saying:
Be still. Watch. Listen.
You are perfectly imperfect.

The cool ribbons wrap around my body
and those tiny feathers transform
into the wings of a great condor.
With these wings, I can take up space —
they spread the width of a canyon.

I dismount the rocky edge
catching the wind
I take flight.

SUNTALKING by Natalie Keshlear

Early morning, I talk with sun.

Do me a favor —
take this smallness,
this self-hate and unworthiness.

Blow kisses into it, so fiery.
Love it right.
Burning it up like ash.

Mix it with red clay, mud
and create up-power.
Smooth out the edges with care.

Sun makes the day new.

I'm giving the moments
of ghostlike otherness a new name:
Not mine.

Take this pain and change its name to grief
and fully know how wonderful it is to feel.

Give aloneness a new name too, solitude.
Understand love is where I stand —
red mud-caked feet and all.

I step out, tall, with sequoia-like tenderness.
I will be exactly as powerful as I can imagine.

Smoke signals lead me home.
Wind whispering "you belong."
Join me.

Great Butterfly Being

Today you will meet the Great Butterfly Being who will help
you identify and let go of any last dregs of shadow, doubt, fear,
hurt, worry, or wound that keep you small. Then the Great Butterfly Being will gift you their golden wisdom to help you claim
and inhabit your wings, your power, your magic, your life!

Body/Mindfulness: Cozy in and close your eyes. Feel supported by what's underneath and behind you, so you can
soften, deepen, melt open. Allow your breath to breathe you in
waves, filling and emptying you effortlessly. Clear your mind
from the world of things to do and arrive here in the infinite
now. Imagine yourself somewhere in nature that feels safe and
sacred. Sit or lie down, and thank the earth and the elements.
Thank the life force. Now welcome the Great Butterfly Being
who is approaching to bring you into their clan and offer support and wisdom. Notice what they look like, their energy,
how they move and communicate, how it feels to be in their
presence. Allow them to help you dissolve any last dregs that
keep you small. Thank them. Stand tall now as they bow and

touch you with their sensitive antennae, conveying precious wisdom and activating your wings. Give yourself time to absorb this experience. When you've received your message and you feel your wings unfurling vibrant and strong, thank the Great Butterfly Being, breathe into your wings, and return by gently opening your eyes.

WRITE NOW! *Write about your experience with the Great Butterfly Being. What did they look like? How did you feel in their presence? How did they communicate with you? What did they help you let go of, and what wisdom did they share with you? How does it feel to receive your wings? Keep breathing into those wings.*

Examples

WAKE UP by Liz Kughn

> I felt you tapping on my left shoulder
> and woke to find myself in your mirror
> my lost words now coming to me.
>
> A quiet storm
> with wind and rain slamming
> against the side of my house.
> *Wake up! Wake up!* you said,
> and I did, your words
> like a trail of breadcrumbs
> leading me home.
>
> *Let go!* you said,
> let the past fall away
> like shards of broken glass.

First find the center and stay there, breathing,
then safety will come knocking at your door.
Let me in! she will say, but she is not an intruder.

I pause, knowing that I must welcome her in.
This is the gift you've been waiting for, she says
extending her long, beautiful arms toward me.
You already have what it takes, she says,
but you have to let go of false stories
no matter how accurate they are in the telling.

You must tell a new story
weave a new tapestry
full of color and magic
like a beacon of light shimmering
across a dark sea.

This means risking the discovery
that I am not alone
and that the worst is over.
There is pain in this potion
and the journey is not for the faint of heart.

But I am flying, my wings stretched wide
over farmland, deserts, rivers, and streams
flowers pushing out
through cracks and crevices
in all corners of the earth.

Now I am laughing
tears running down my face
as my own true longing overtakes me
I am the minister of my own soul.

I am a seeker
one who knows
both weight and weightlessness.

I am still my mother's daughter
but I am no longer her prisoner.
I can speak words of love and mean them
allowing my hunger to be my guide.

BLUE MORPHO by Nicole Phillips

She graced me
in the early morning
a floating flash
a bold burlesque dancer
wrapped in a blue scarf
circus star of the jungle.
Accompanied by an orchestra
of cicadas, frogs, scarlet macaws,
howler monkeys, toucans,
Oropendola
keeping the thick pulse.
I am entranced
as she bursts through
the sound score
with a wisp of metallic blue
sparkles of fairy dust
tease behind her,
her voice is her flight.
She splashes
giant waxy-green
jungle leaves with
her hot-blue paint

then comes to rest
her black string legs
on my green bamboo
shorts' pocket
seasoned with jungle scents
I haven't washed for days.
I gaze into her
toasted wooden
brown underwing
as she masquerades
as tree notches
their fourteen eyes
stare back at me.
Flares of blue flaming magic
on one side,
earth on the other side,
transformation
doesn't have to
be traumatic.
She stays on my clothes
for a whole blessed minute —
"Blend in when you need to," she says.
  "Be still,
    then razzle-dazzle life
      with a striking color.
Your color is your voice."

Song of the Butterfly

You have arrived. *You* are now the Great Butterfly Being, winged and wondrous. It's time for you, beautiful, powerful, magician of metamorphosis, to share your song. Your song integrates what you have learned while journeying from egg to butterfly. Soon you will meet back up with the Great Butterfly Clan to share what you've learned about yourself, your journey, and your relationship with change. Who are you now, and how do you show up with yourself and life? How do you embody and dance with change? How do you feed your heart, fuel your wings, power your passion and purpose? What is your nectar? What is your song?

Body/Mindfulness: Settle in and close the wings of your eyes. Find your breath and arrive. Take a seat in the center of your being. Imagine that the Great Butterfly Being who came forth to help guide you is now sitting beside you. I want you to do something wild: step right into the center of this great butterfly and become it. Don't think; just do it. Feel your body merge with its body. Feel your wings grow wide and strong and beautiful as you begin to flutter, a fully empowered empress, magician of metamorphosis. Feel into what you've learned about yourself during your journey of change. What is your wisdom, Great Butterfly?

WRITE NOW! *Write about how it feels to be the Great Butterfly. What's it like to open your wings? What have you learned about dancing with change? Share your wisdom with the clan. Sing your song of change, wisdom, power, life!*

Examples

MY INTUITION IS A BUTTERFLY by Tanya Flanagin

> My intuition is a butterfly
> wrapped in silk

silver and blue
my soft underbelly
filled with the wisdom
of the moon's cycles
the ebb and flow
when to start, when to finish
my ancestors' song.

Wings formed from
a brilliant knowing
that the flight of change
is possibility or pain
sometimes both.

This audacious knowing
teaches me
that fear wants me
and the more I run
she runs faster.

She comes closer
beating like a heart
that thumps me awake
in my darkest nights.

Yes, it's true, fear wants me
but not in the way I have imagined
her true desire is to know me.

Now for the first time
I want to know her too.
I invite her on this journey

of becoming,
this silver and blue
beauty in my gut
teaching me
that messy is OK
struggle can be trusted
not knowing
where I'm going
can be the right path.

Mystery is a map
and faith
my copilot.

BIRTHING BALANCE by Beatrix Bliss

Who knew
my coming-out party
would be so full,
of stillness.

No bells
and whistles.
No glitz,
or glitter,
but silence.

An all-pervading
silence.
In darkness,
in the womb.

In the vastness
of darkness,

a drop
a pearl
a pinprick
a great big
aha.
So this —
this is what all the fuss is about?

Not glamorous
or even
adventurous.
No ego trip,
or sergeant's whip.
No right or wrong
or dance,
or song.

Just
all-pervading
velvet-textured
embrace.
The feeling of being held,
contained
alongside the sense
of unlimited potential.
A never-ending sequence
of possibilities
rippling out
unencumbered.

Held,
not trapped.
Vast,

untethered.
not lost at sea
but somewhere
softly stretched out
in the middle.

Like how a tree
grows simultaneously
down and under
as well as
up and out.
Roots and branch,
earth and sky.

To fly
you need to know:
not merely
how to take off,
but also
how to land,
and when.

Gone are the days
of launching off
into oblivion,
only to see
what would happen next.

Here are the ways
of sensing, feeling,
discerning.
Moving with,

not against.
Alongside,
not in front
or behind.

Swimming through earth.
Flying through water.
Held in air.
Rooted in fire.
An elemental sandwich.

So now that you feel
the wings
that were there
all along,
notice the gravity
in your toes
before you take off.
And then notice how
your expansion
roots to ground.

This is balance.
And balance
is not boring.
Balance
is boundless.

Conclusion

I started Writing by Heart poetry workshops during the pandemic with just a handful of women from Marin County, California. Now people from all over the world attend every series and return with their friends. We have writers in the UK, France, the Netherlands, and New Zealand. There's a woman in Egypt who wakes up at 1 a.m. to Zoom with us. Another in Croatia who stays up all night to join us. I Zoom with groups of incarcerated women in prison. Women from Nova Scotia, Hawaii, Alaska, and all across the US come to write at the hearth of our circle.

I have the honor and joy of guiding and supporting these amazing human beings as they write their way to the clarity and courage it takes to change careers, retire, go back to school, end unfulfilling relationships, choose for or against having a baby, birth a new project, meet their next soul mate, explore gender and sexuality choices, devote themselves to a cause, make peace with loss, navigate illness and injury, grieve the death of a loved one, unravel and integrate their past, learn to trust their heart, dream themselves anew. They tell me that they walk their workshop experience into their lives, standing taller and truer, saying yes when they mean yes and no when they mean no. They are able to access a source of wisdom that comes from their writing and from the support of the group. I can hear it in their poems, can't you?

And do you hear it in *your* poems now that you've written your way through some or most of this book? Deep bow to you, warrior poet. You are now one of us. I'm curious — how was your experience? Did you learn to trust the writing process? Ever feel that the poem knows the poem? Have any magic moments when you touched your truth and tapped your wild wisdom? Write any pieces you love? I hope so. I hope writing has become a lifeline, haven, and companion for you the way it has for me and for so many of my students. I invite you to keep writing! This book is a wellspring that won't run dry. Dip back into any of the writing invitations, and work with them again and again for anything and everything that's happening in your life. There is always more to uncover and discover, layer by layer, breath by breath, word by word. Writing is an alchemical process in which we take the raw material of our lives and transform it into something vital and luminous.

If you'd like more support, please join our growing garden of writers by registering for one of my upcoming workshops. We'd love to have you! Until then, may the stories, poems, and songs of your life bloom in ways that heal and nourish you as you write yourself home to your wild and tender heartland.

Love and Gratitude

Huge gratitude to Georgia Hughes and Marc Allen at New World Library for believing in me twice, two books! Extra special thanks to Georgia Hughes for loving the example poems in this book as much as I do and for guiding me in how to make the introduction sing. For my editors, Kristen Cashman and Mimi Kusch, for tending to each and every word in my book with the deepest care and respect. Thank you to my agent, Patrick Miller, who took a chance on me, and we both discovered he was right! Thanks to my new friend, John Fox, founder of the Institute for Poetic Medicine, who teaches me what kindness feels like. To my mother, there is not yet a word invented to express my love for you. To my bestie, Annelies Atchley, you are my rock. To my river tribe: Chula, Lauren, Victoria, Indigo, Veronica, Dave, and Jan, for always lending a willing ear to my river love poems. And finally, immense love and respect to you, the women poets who show up each week in workshop and bring it. You inspire us all to be wildly, truthfully alive.

Poems by Chapter

All student poetry used with permission.

Chapter 2: Elemental Wisdom

EARTH by Nicole Phillips
EARTH by Lisa Eddy
THE AIR AT DUSK by Ani Meier
THE UPDRAFT by Tiffany Fyans
FLAMES by Lindsay Chinapen
FIRE by Mary Pritchard
WONDROUS WATER by Jeannie McKenzie
WATER I AM by Nicole Phillips
I AM EARTH by Kelli Mulligan
I AM AIR by Laurie McMillan
I AM FIRE by Natalie Keshlear
I AM WATER by Verana Bailowitz

Chapter 3: Body Language

MY HANDS by Heather Irene Bush
THE HAND I WAS DEALT by Heleen Ellmore-Walzer
BUDDHA BELLY by Indigo Donaldson
PURGING FALSEHOODS by Heleen Ellmore-Walzer
WHAT'S BETWEEN US by Natalie Keshlear
BLOOMING HIPS by Lindsay Chinapen
DRAGON SPINE by Jeannie McKenzie
THANK YOU, BODY by Hala Emad
V by Dawn Li

Chapter 4: Sensorium

Chapter 5: Wild Heart

Chapter 6: Sanctuary

Chapter 7: Belonging

Chapter 10: Bloom

SPRING by Dawn Li
SPRING by Jeannie McKenzie
RHYTHMS OF DIRT by Ann McGuire
DIRT by Verana Bailowitz
BLOOMERS by Meredith Heller
GARDEN VARIETY by Jac-Lynn Stark
BEIGE PANTIES by Teddi Dysart
SAILING by Mireya Quirie
AURORA BLOOMS by Dawn Li
GROUP BLOOM
BLOSSOM OF INFINITE CHANGE by Karen Burt-Imira
BIRTHDAY BLOOM by Verana Bailowitz

Chapter 11: Zen Bones

CIRCLE OF SEVEN by Jo Walker
FAITH & FOG by Karen Burt-Imira
TOASTING THE MOON by Jac-Lynn Stark
GRANDMOTHER MOON by Verana Bailowitz
CATERPILLAR GIRL by Meredith Heller
JELLYFISH by Nicole Phillips
SNAKE FRIEND by Jessica Ulrich
WATER PRAYER by Mireya Quirie
RAINY SEASON by Nicole Phillips
BONES by Jo Walker
BONE SONG by Meredith Heller
MEMENTO AMARI, MEMENTO VIVERE by Trisha Coghlan

Chapter 12: Heartbeat

MY HEARTBEAT by Korynn Amm
SOFT HEART by Kathryn Thompson
HEARTBEATS REMEMBERED by Linda B.

Chapter 13: Moon Dance

Chapter 14: Metamorphosis

Index of Poets

Some poets are identified with first name and last-name initial only to respect their privacy.

Amm, Korynn *Chesterton, IN*
Asana of Belonging, 160
My Heartbeat, 243
Ripe Fruit, 172
Rust, 192

B., Linda
Heartbeats Remembered, 246

Bailowitz, Verana *Richmond, CA*
Birthday Bloom, 218
Dirt, 205
Grandmother Moon, 225
Grandmother Whale, 253
Holy Purple Gardeners, 273
I Am Water, 31
Moon Bear, 270
My Tush & I, 72

Barber, Sarah *Milwaukee, WI*
Little Anchors, 56
My Breasts, 59

Barerra, Shankari Linda *Portland, OR*
This Arrow, 187

About the Author

Meredith Heller is a poet, author, singer/songwriter, avid nature lover, and educator with degrees in writing and education. A California Poet in the Schools, she leads workshops at public and private schools, women's prisons, the Institute for Poetic Medicine, creativity summits, wellness retreats, and online. Her passion is empowering people to believe in themselves, trust their creative instincts, tap their wild wisdom, express their truth, and ignite their hearts. Her poems and essays appear in numerous literary collections. She is the author of *Write a Poem, Save Your Life* and three poetry collections, *Songlines*, *Yuba Witch*, and *River Spells*. She lives with a gentle footprint in Northern California. Join her for a workshop: MeredithHeller.com.

NEW WORLD LIBRARY is dedicated to publishing books and other media that inspire and challenge us to improve the quality of our lives and the world.

We are a socially and environmentally aware company. We recognize that we have an ethical responsibility to our readers, our authors, our staff members, and our planet.

We serve our readers by creating the finest publications possible on personal growth, creativity, spirituality, wellness, and other areas of emerging importance. We serve our authors by working with them to produce and promote quality books that reach a wide audience. We serve New World Library employees with generous benefits, significant profit sharing, and constant encouragement to pursue their most expansive dreams.

Whenever possible, we print our books with soy-based ink on 100 percent postconsumer-waste recycled paper. We power our Northern California office with solar energy, and we respectfully acknowledge that it is located on the ancestral lands of the Coast Miwok Indians. We also contribute to nonprofit organizations working to make the world a better place for us all.

Our products are available wherever books are sold.

customerservice@NewWorldLibrary.com
Phone: 415-884-2100 or 800-972-6657
Orders: Ext. 110
Fax: 415-884-2199
NewWorldLibrary.com

Scan below to access our newsletter
and learn more about our books and authors.